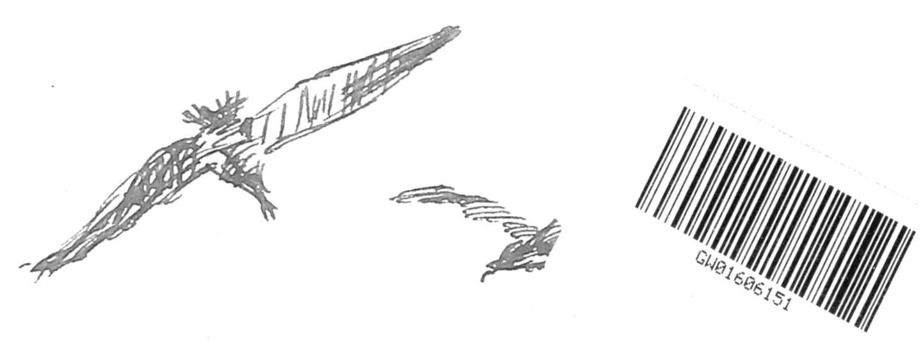

Celebration

A COLLECTION OF PAINTINGS BY TED DYER

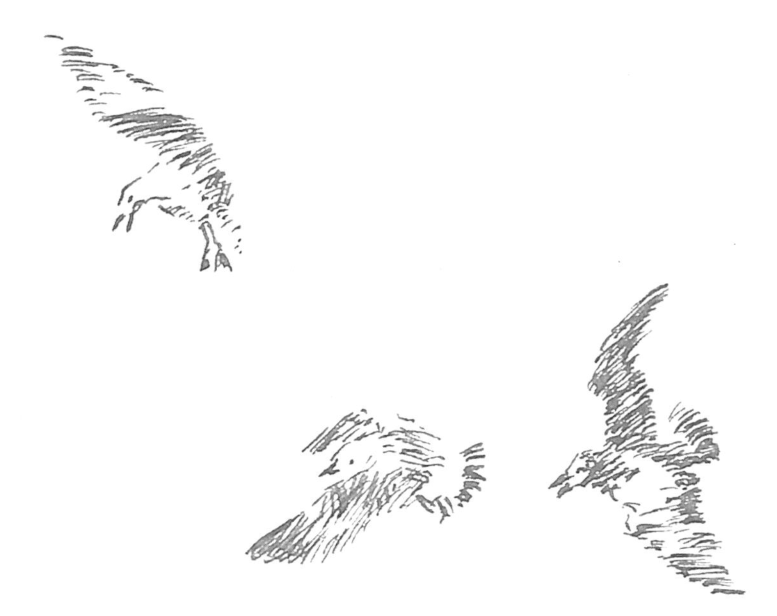

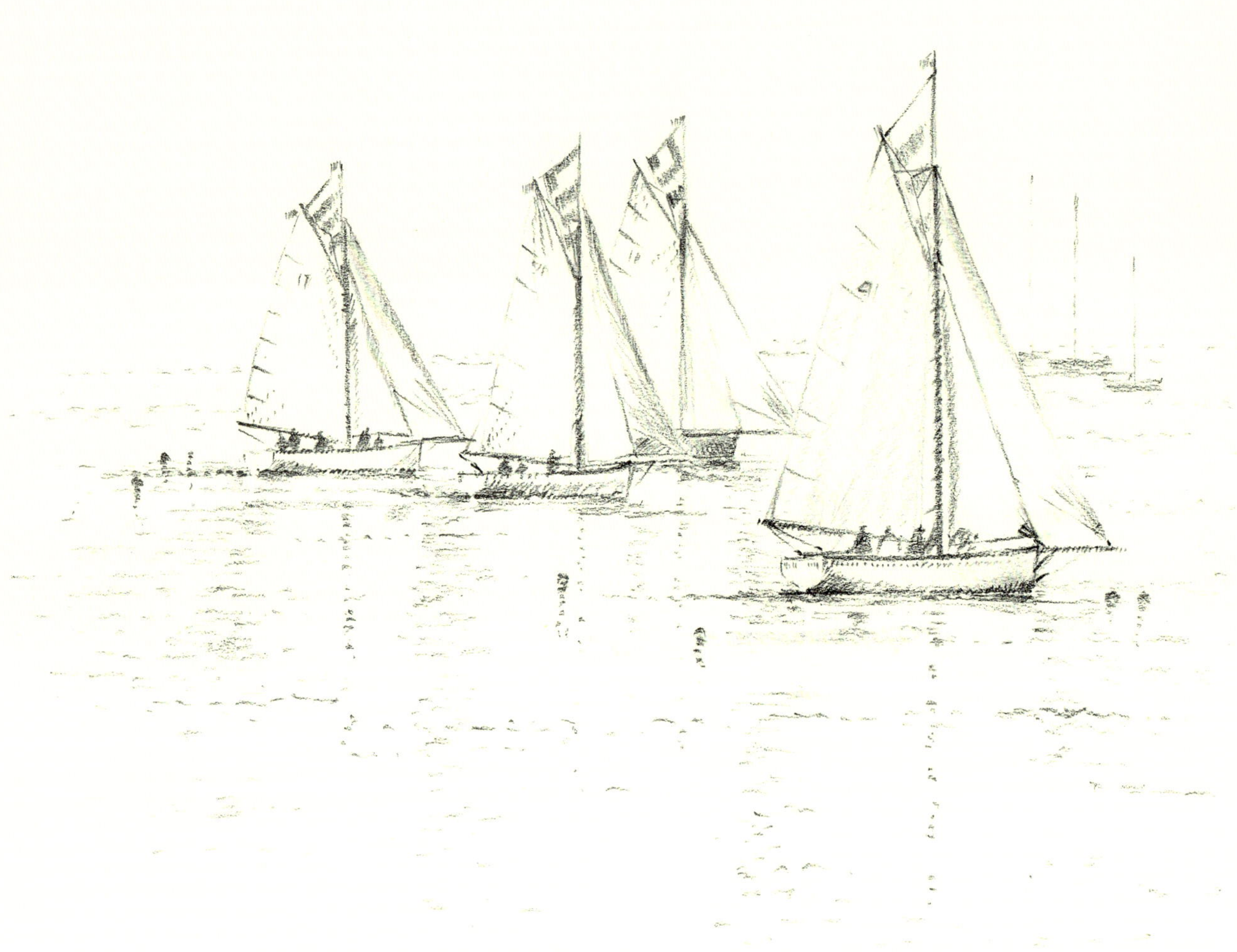

Celebration is a collection of paintings by the artist Ted Dyer. For the first time he has set down in words his feelings and experiences in conjunction with his paintings. His writing conveys his love of Cornwall and draws on events encountered in his everyday life. He brings to our attention the places which are of most importance to him, which include the harbour and beaches at Falmouth, the creeks of Helford and the cliffs around Zennor. His personal narrative is a delight to read and provides collectors and admirers of his work with a unique insight into his thoughts and inspirations.

In this catalogue Ted introduces us to many new and exciting subjects which have provided him with new challenges during the past two years. It contains subjects which will be familiar to those who know his work well but he has approached these paintings with new ideas and a fresh outlook. There are several major groupings of paintings in this selection of particular interest: his Nocturne series including the Proms in the Park, fireworks at Falmouth and the bandstand, his paintings at Priest's Cove, and his series of creek paintings. Some of these paintings, especially the larger ones, are real landmarks in Ted's development as an artist. He has achieved paintings of true excellence, drawing on his skill as a painter acquired over many years.

"Proms in the Park, Lanhydrock" is a very exciting change of subject matter which Ted has translated into a fantastic painting full of atmosphere and glowing light, which leaps out from the canvas. In this painting and even more evidently in *"Proms in the Park, Finale"* he has skillfully placed small areas of colour which when viewed at close quarters are almost a random pattern to the eye, but on stepping back from the painting, they so naturally fall into place to form the coherent structure of the illuminated crowd.

Ted's decision to paint a Triptych, *"Festival of Fireworks, Falmouth"* was a brilliant idea to compose the panoramic view from Flushing to Customs House Quay. Although each canvas is a separate work and can be viewed individually, the eye quite naturally scans the three separate images and combines them as a whole. He has inlaid gold leaf on to the surface of the canvas to enhance the sparks and luminescence from the fireworks adding an exciting new dimension to his work.

"A Midsummer's Night Performance" is another incredible piece of work with a balance between structure, detail and lighting holding together perfectly in a truly magical painting. One can almost feel the atmosphere of the hushed silence of the onlookers as the band plays.

The Priest's Cove oils capture the strength and movement of a continually changing subject, the sea. One of the most challenging subjects to paint but handled in these paintings with great confidence and skill. In contrast in his creek series of paintings he has portrayed the still and tranquil quality of the water as can be seen in *"High Tide on a Glorious Day"*. In these paintings as with many in this collection he has used carefully chosen figures in his compositions, these give his paintings not only added interest but also a sense of scale and a narrative theme. He often uses family and close friends as reference as well as using figures he sees in naturally occurring situations, such as in *"Playing in the Pool above Mermaid's Cove, Zennor"*.

This really must be Ted Dyer's most exciting collection of work to date, conveying his true passion for Cornwall. The catalogue includes illustrations of watercolours and oil sketches as well as major works on canvas and has been produced in a limited number, which we are sure will become truly collectable in years to come.

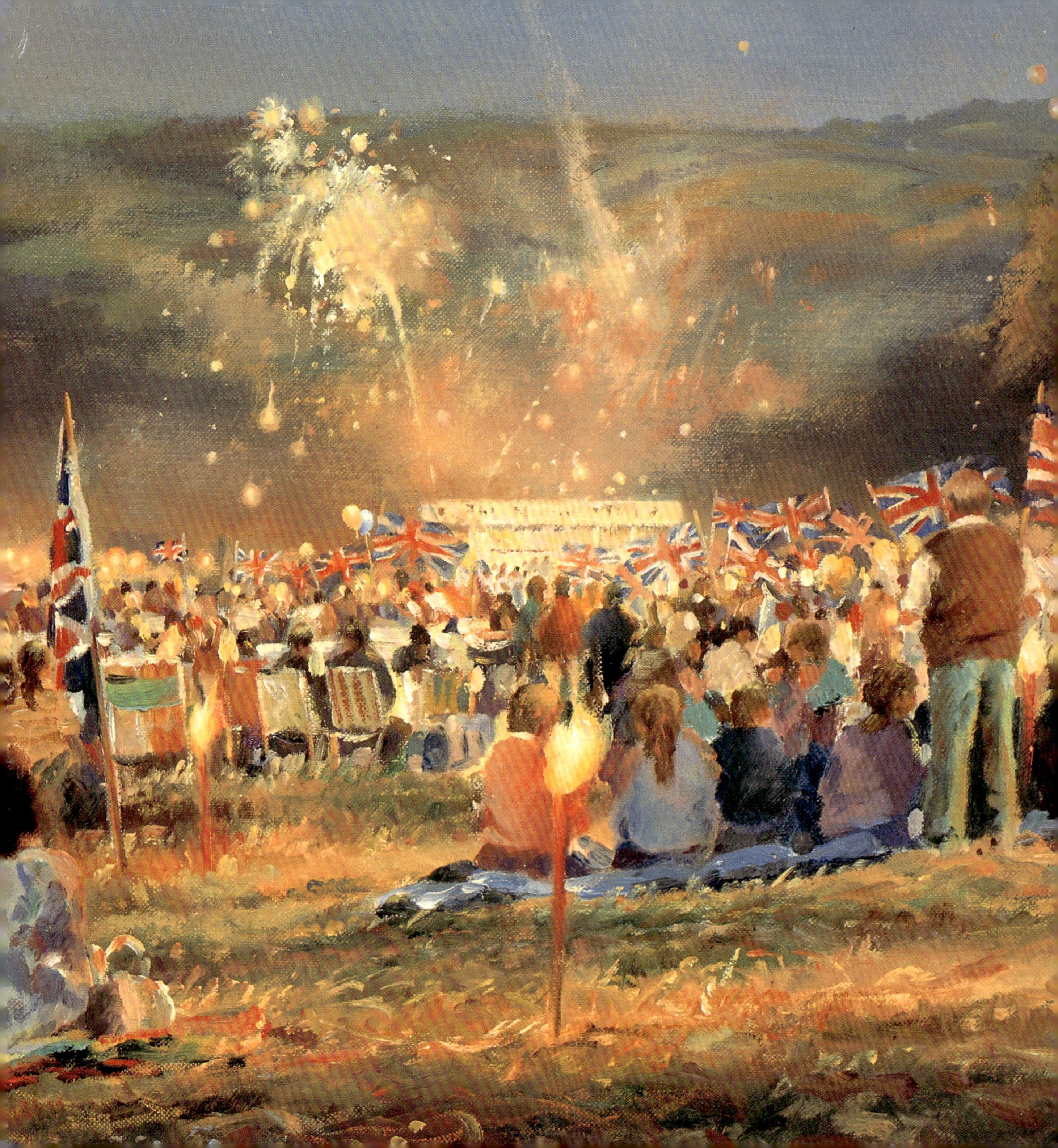

ANOTHER YEAR has passed and with it many of my best intentions. Perhaps as today is my birthday inevitably there is a little soul searching and therefore this might be a good opportunity to reflect on the subject of time. It really does not seem like two years since my last exhibition at Beside The Wave, and although the work spans that period, now that I look at the stacked canvases and sheets of watercolours I wonder at the ratio of time and effort to finished work. Has the pace of life got faster, more demanding, or is it, as I suspect, that the younger you are the more time there is ?

I RECALL THE days spent waiting for the right light, the right tide and then setting off only to find that true to its nature, Cornwall is as nowhere else. It may be the right light and mist combination here in Falmouth, but say at Zennor, the mist has probably long gone, to be replaced by dazzling sunlight that turns the crystal clear sea to such an intense shade of turquoise that if painted accurately, or as accurately as pigments and skill allow, would approach reality and not be believed. 'Nature up to her old tricks again.

The *ebauche* or laying in at the start of a painting is critical, somewhat akin to chess I feel, in that the strategy has to be thought about and if moves ahead can not be foreseen then the result is often to one's disadvantage. Maybe not defeat, but certainly a compromise over original intentions. For me the start of any painting requires many decisions; what is to be left in or out, the colour and tonal range to try to capture a little of not only the visual components, but also and maybe more importantly, the ambience, the very touch and smell, if possible, of the landscape and the conditions it was undergoing that day. For it is the interplay of all the elements that give rise to feelings and emotions, the heart, or so it should be, of any creative work. The uncountable brush strokes which slowly build up the image on the canvas, although individual and sometimes at variance with each other, come together to form an underlying truth, a whole which when viewed together is as near reality as the painter can achieve.

Always though there are new challenges, a particular nuance of light across a scene, a really sparkling sea, a misty cliff say at the Crowns, Botallack, or a nocturne. Nocturne? Well the sky on a summer night can be so so magical and the blue so very far away and yet so close and intense, with the stars increasing the more one looks. Absolutely impossible to paint, and yet the challenge is there. But how ? Even an hour changes one's depth of perception. From early on when there is light to the horizon and fields can clearly be seen in their summer ochres and dull greens, to the deep velvet period does not take long, that is to a painter trying to capture a moment or perhaps a mixture of time lapses to produce a final result. So quick. Not if lying amongst the grasses staring upwards, that would seem forever, but quick, whatever the medium, for a painter. Concentration then, and time stands still until the clock says otherwise.

So when tackling evening subjects the brush strokes do merge to give, in the studio, a remembered vision of that time. This was the case last summer when a combination of July perfectness, a wondrously still night and a clear sky came together in the mildness of a parkland setting on the occasion of a musical performance, ending with a firework display. Well then, what more could a painter desire? Walton, Vaughan-Williams, Parry's Jerusalem and of course that most English of finales, Edward Elgar's Pomp and Circumstance (Land of Hope and Glory). The most English of English occasions with everyone at their best, on their own territory (be it only 6ft square) some with tables, all with picnics, most with winc and many burning torches. The reflective glow so soft and embracing that modern illumination had no place amongst this sort of magic.

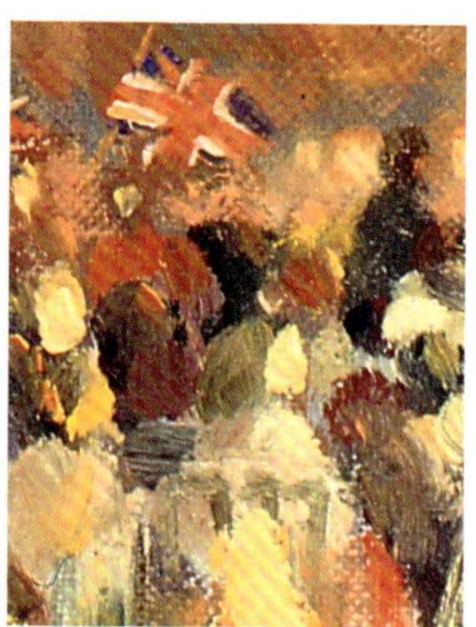

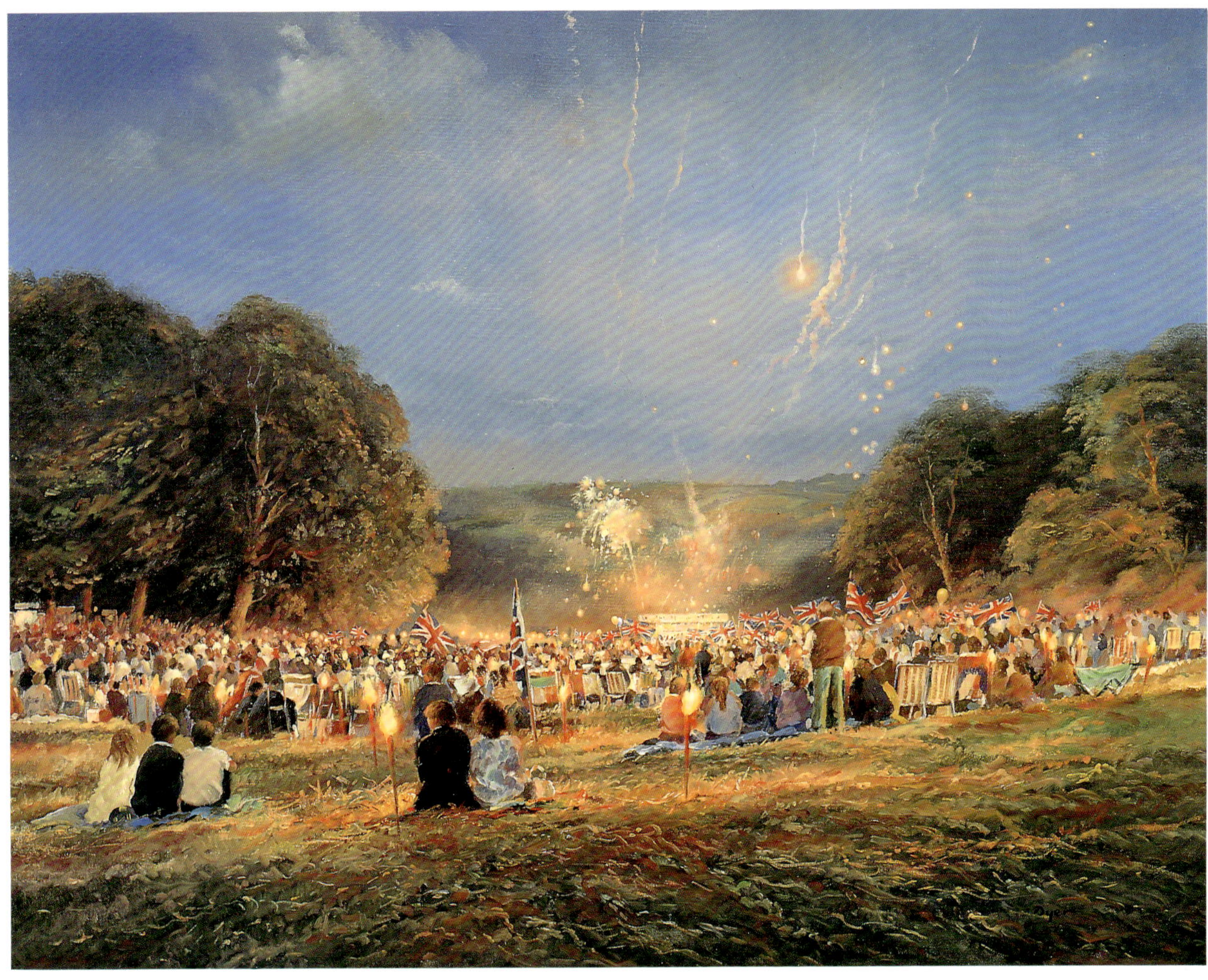

Nocturne: Proms in the Park, Lanhydrock
28 x 36 inches, oil on canvas

Left & Page 4: Detail of, Proms in the Park Lanhydrock

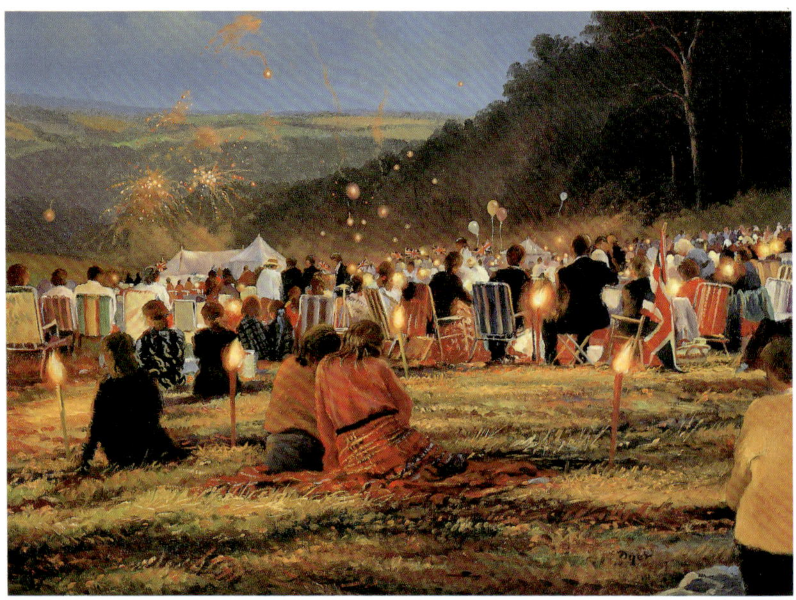

Nocturne: Proms in the Park, Intermission
16 x 22 inches, oil on canvas

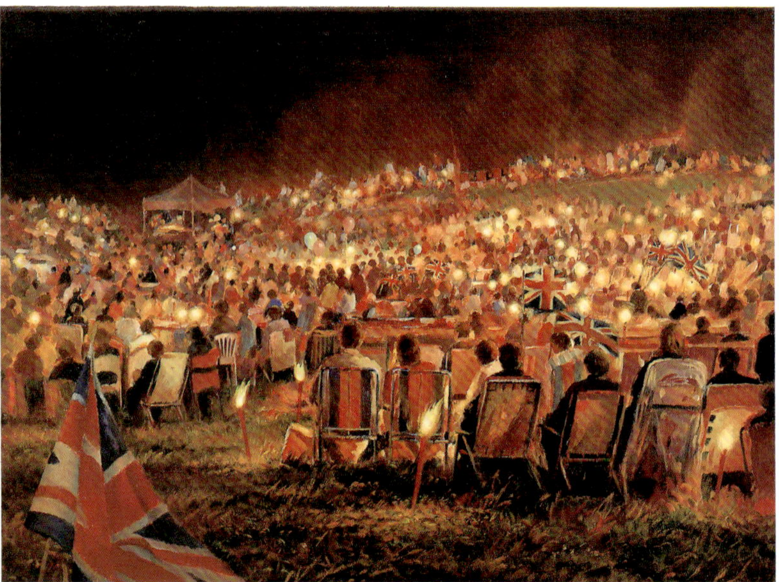

Nocturne: Proms in the Park, Finale
16 x 22 inches, oil on canvas

The music soared, the assembled prom goers swayed, the torches blazed, all with a gentle wave like movement in time with the baton. Union Jacks flew in the night air with a feeling of great unity, as if a long lost tribe had come together. If seen from above it must have seemed as if an important summer ritual, a solstice perhaps, was about to be witnessed. Instead of which Wagnerian like rockets flew and stars burst in a blaze of light and colour. Overhead tracers of red and blue seemed to encompass the sky and then fall quietly away. Perhaps if another musical analogy can be visualised, just when a gentle rhythm was established then Mahlerian forces played with the senses as thunder-flashes shook the stillness. Suddenly, as always happens, it was over.

As I write this I am reminded also of gulls, gulls and rockets and flares, but to link these requires stepping sideways in time.

My studio overlooks the sea and beyond to Roseland where I imagine I can see the little church at St Just. Not that this sea is the sea in officially defined terms, no, this begins beyond Black Rock Buoy, but a sea full of mostly white boats, often Falmouth working boats, against the backdrop of Trefusis. Some days light splinters off the water, others it is half way house between streaks of colour and flattened areas caused by down-draughts of wind, though never the same twice. Sometimes, and for what seems blissfully long periods it is quite calm, completely calm. This happens more at either end of the day, my favourite being the morning, say at six, when the waterfront is unbelievably still, set in amber and almost with that colour. A moment in time when even the gulls become silent, but not I might add for long. Moving from the sea and towards the middle distance, no-man's land, quite literally, as the rooftops belong to the sea birds. Old roofs these, some with a concrete wash in the Cornish tradition of running repairs and all with the evidence of their occupants. An area of noise as well, especially in the summer when the young begin to appear. Young clowns to eventually join the adult performing troupe, aggressive, noisy and surprisingly big, but undoubtable characters. For normal birds, as I know them, that would be that, but for our population there is a nocturnal habit of night flying. Somewhat disturbingly, and I'm sure to most peoples disbelief, the gulls soar, ghostly white against an indigo sky. Sometimes the odd one or two, mostly many, fly around the church tower like spent rockets or flares, a blur in the night sky before coming to rest and landing noisily to berate their neighbours. Sometimes from the Quay a juxtaposition of the moon, weather and gulls occurs and a full moon, silhouette of the church, and spiralling gulls, with their reflections in the water below, means the spirits of old soar as well. Nature's own prom, with the squawking and screeching below and shooting stars above. A moment in time again, to be remembered and stored, to be replayed with all the imperfections that we fallible humans have. Layer on layer of experience to colour the event and emotions to point the way. But how again to capture on canvas ? Did Whistler come close ? I think he did.

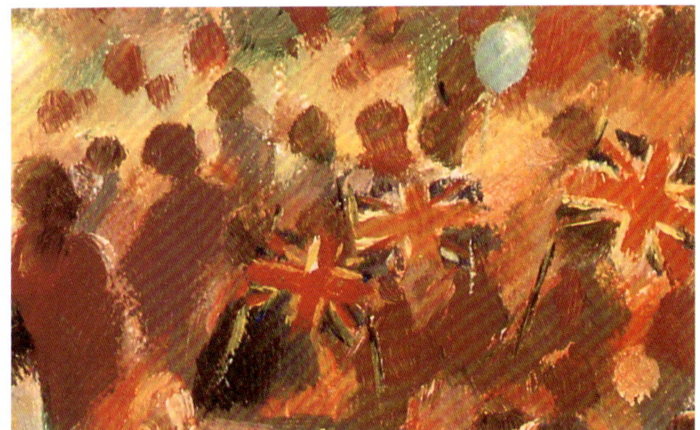

Detail of, Proms in the Park, Finale

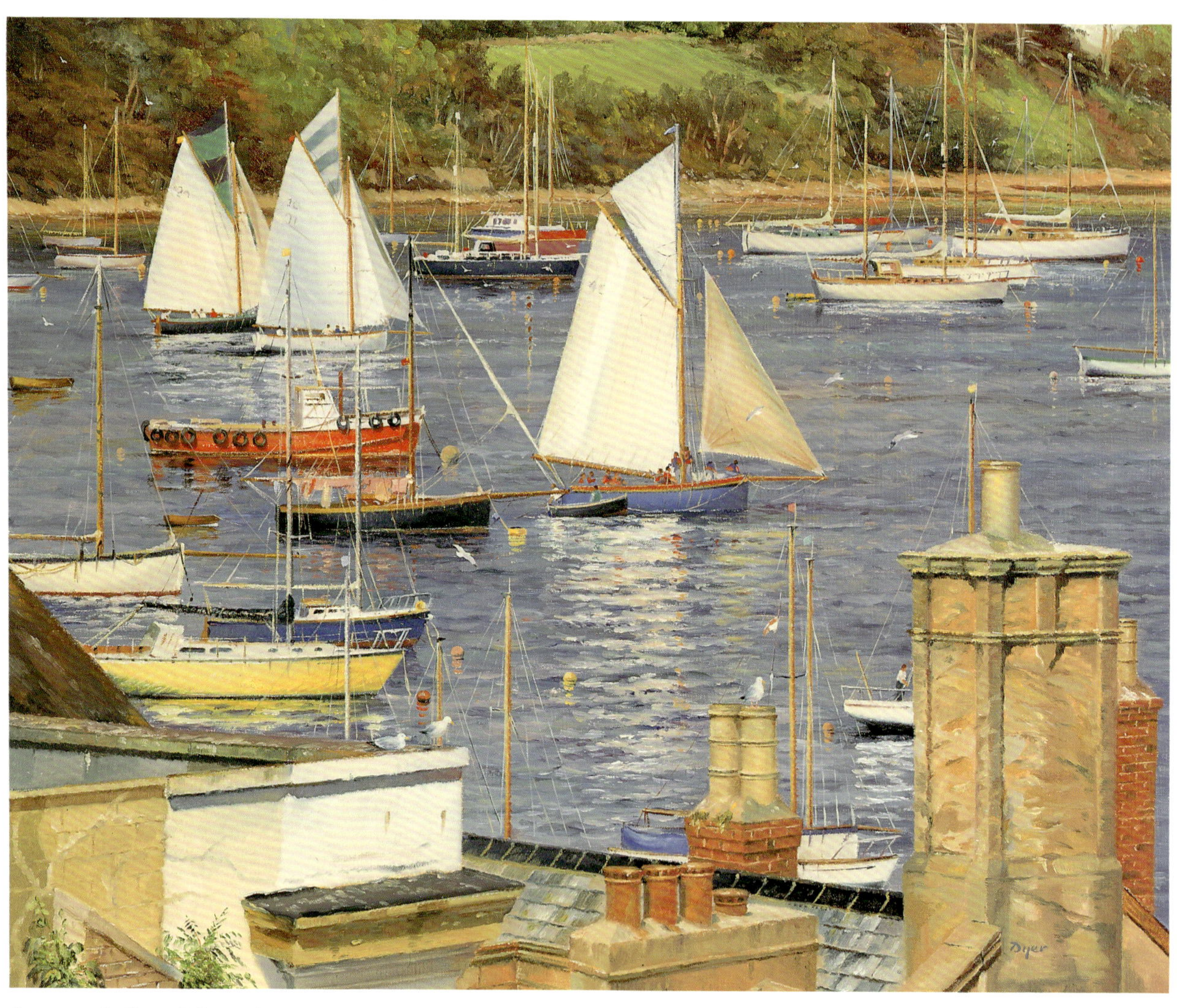

Summer Sailing, Falmouth
20 x 24 inches, oil on canvas

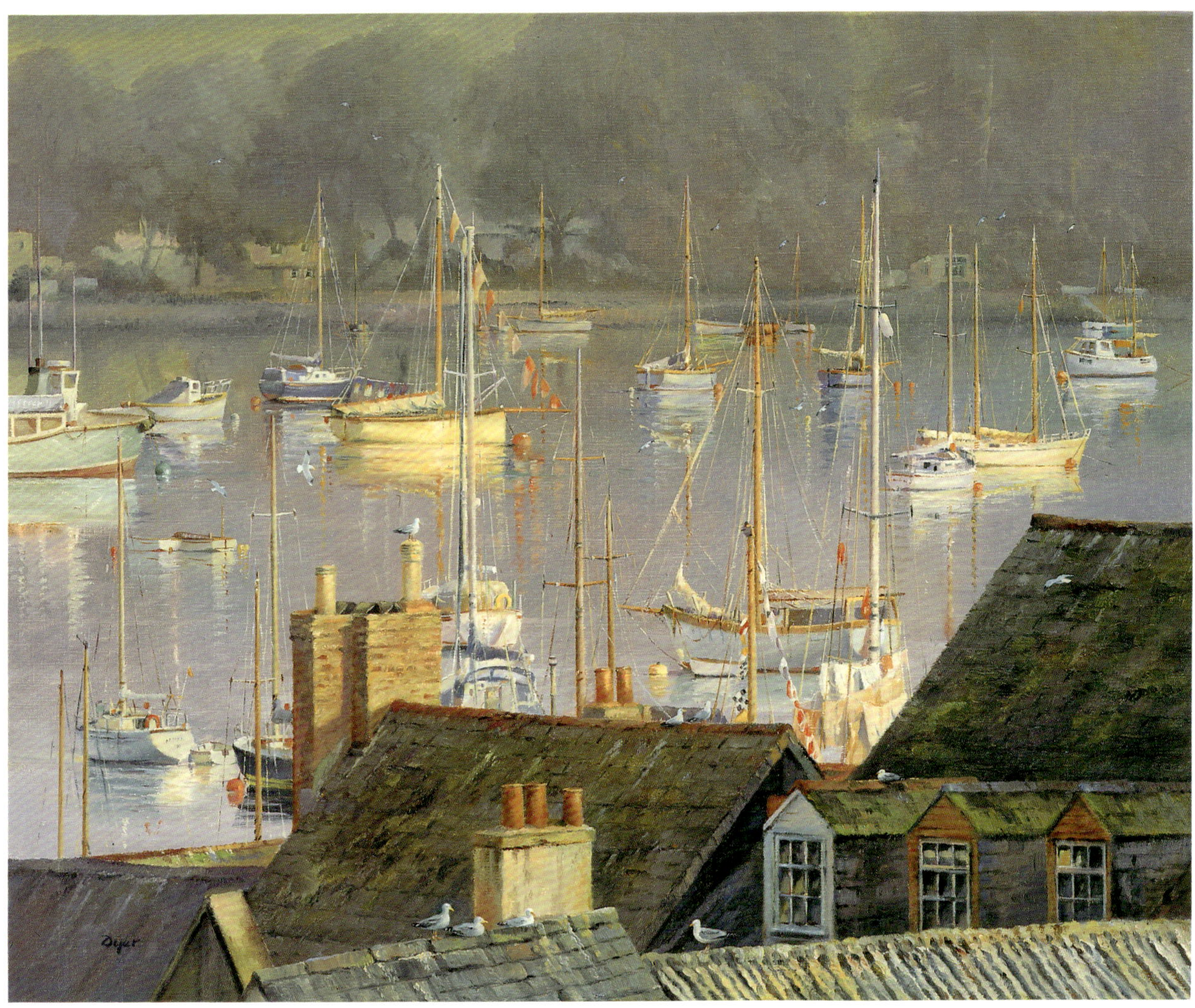

Early Morning Calm, Falmouth Waterfront
24 x 30 inches, oil on canvas

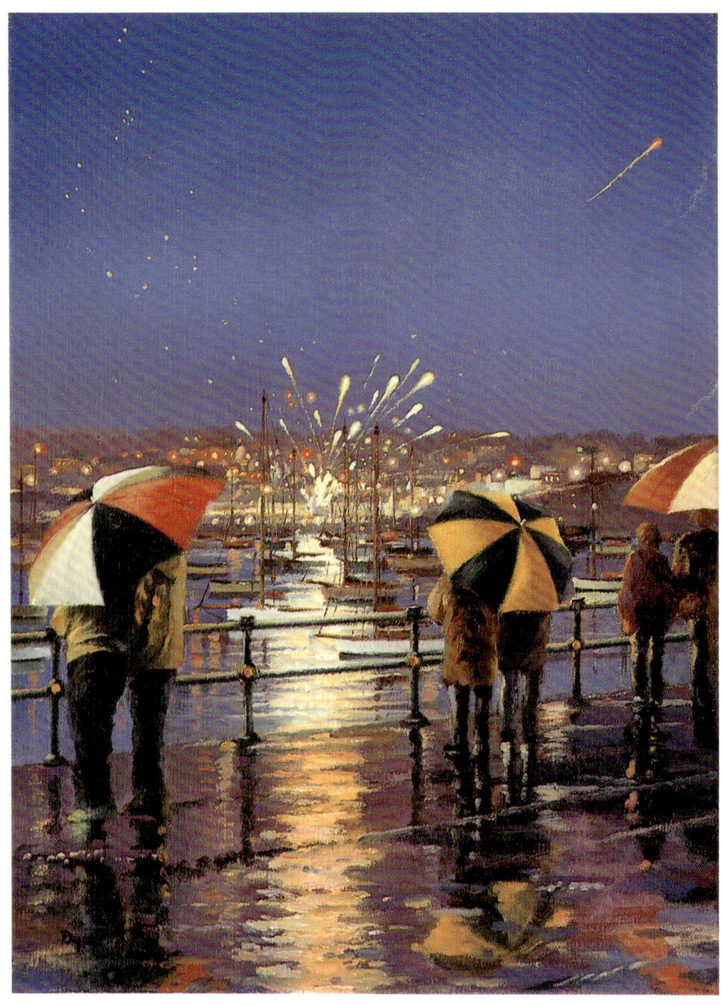

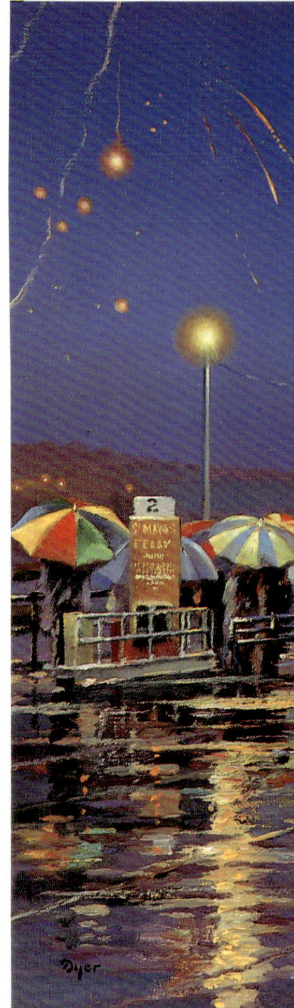

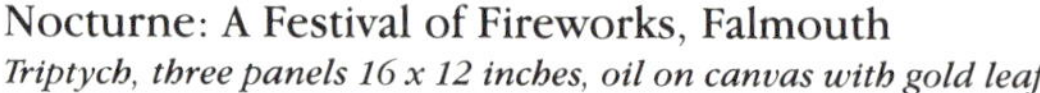

Nocturne: A Festival of Fireworks, Falmouth
Triptych, three panels 16 x 12 inches, oil on canvas with gold leaf

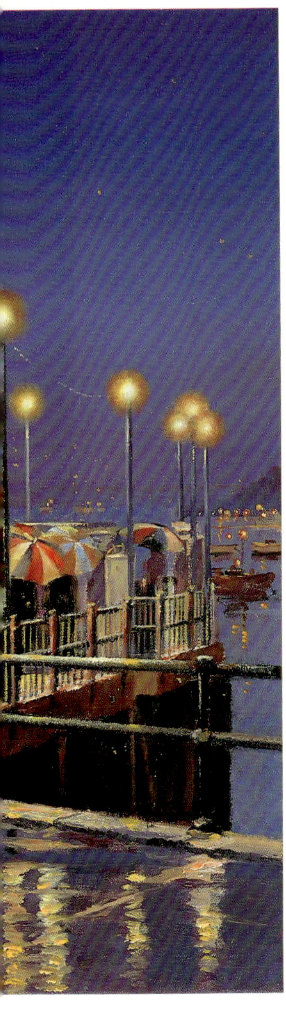

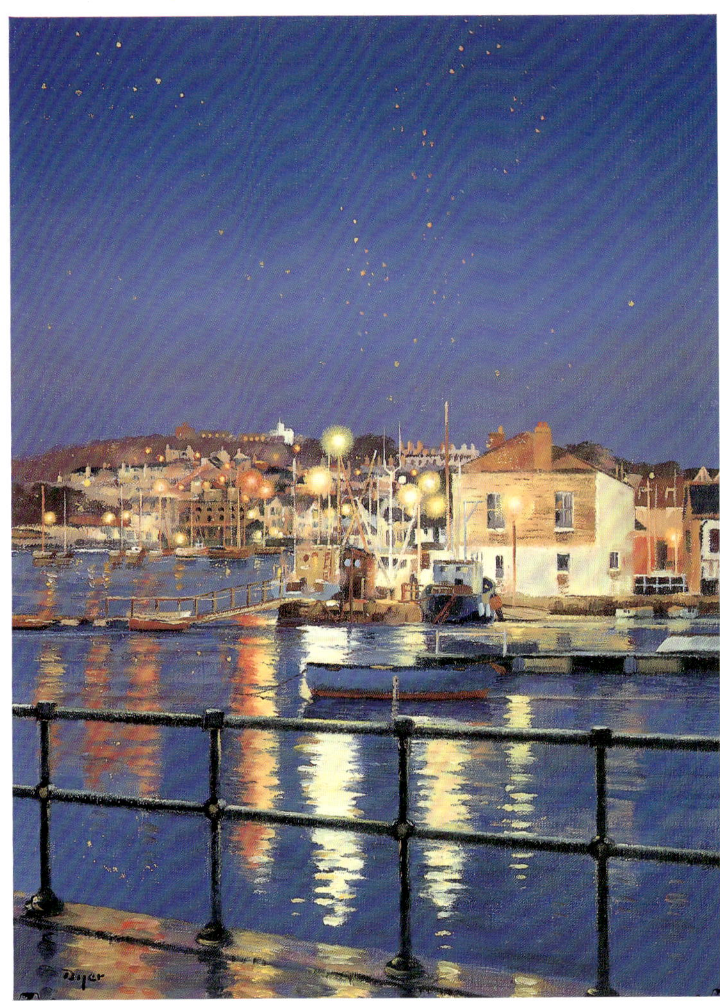

Then the annual fireworks at Falmouth, another traditional but surreal event and this time more so because of rain and reflections. To overcome time differences I decided to opt for a Triptych. Three canvases, each depicting slightly different times and view points but all with a blue and gold leaf theme running through them. Maybe *alla prima* (wet in wet) could have been used for the finished painting, but mostly changes were made during the work and a variety of techniques employed over a period of time.

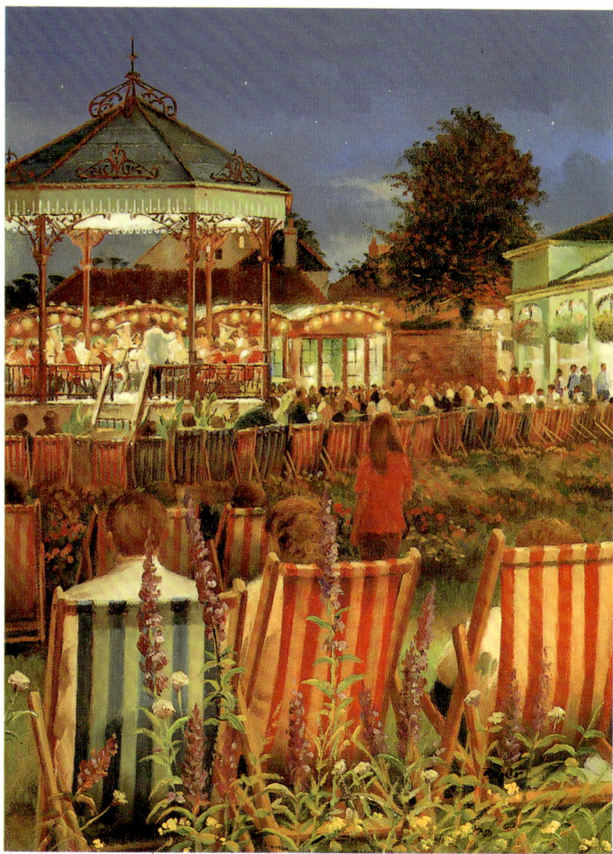

Nocturne: Music under the Stars
16 x 12 inches, oil on canvas

Such was the case in the other Nocturne, depicting the bandstand. Perspective was important but overriding this was the glow from the area of the performers and under the canopy radiating out over the spectators. No rockets this time, but quiet stars to form a silent peaceful backdrop, civilised and structured. I shall remember the bandstand for a long time. Whilst painting it I strived not to loose the important feeling and atmosphere of this memorable event.

Right: Nocturne: A Midsummer's Night Performance, Gyllyngdune Gardens
28 x 36 inches, oil on canvas

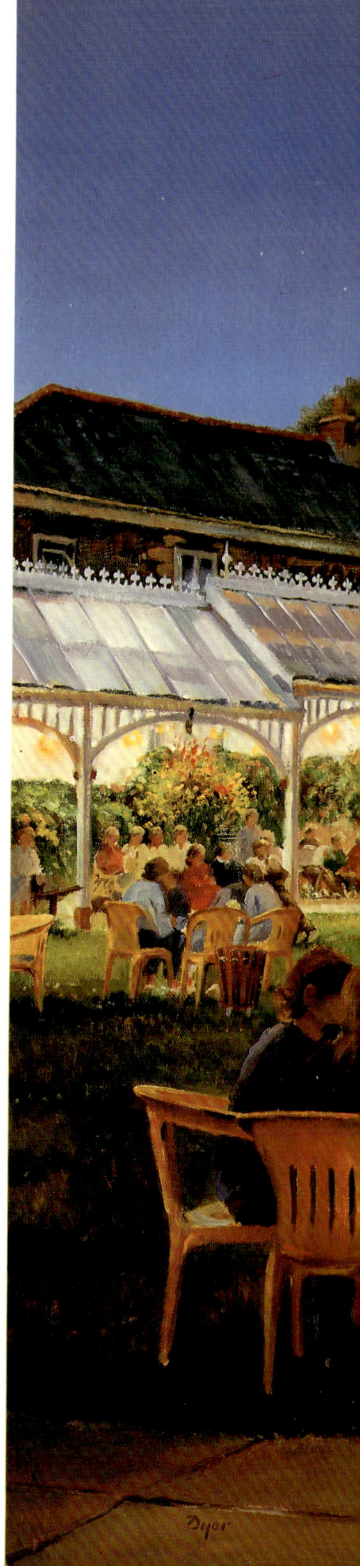

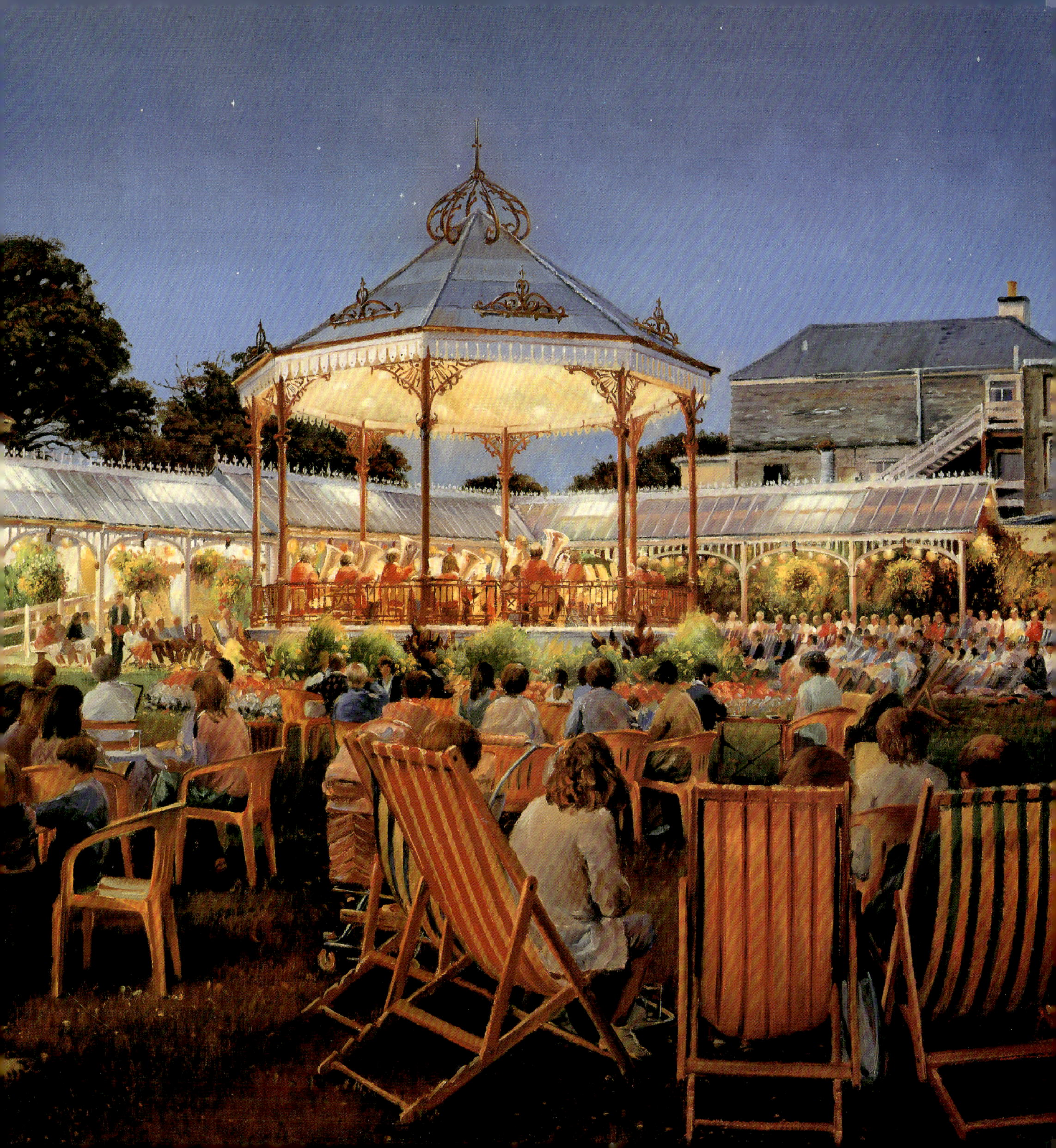

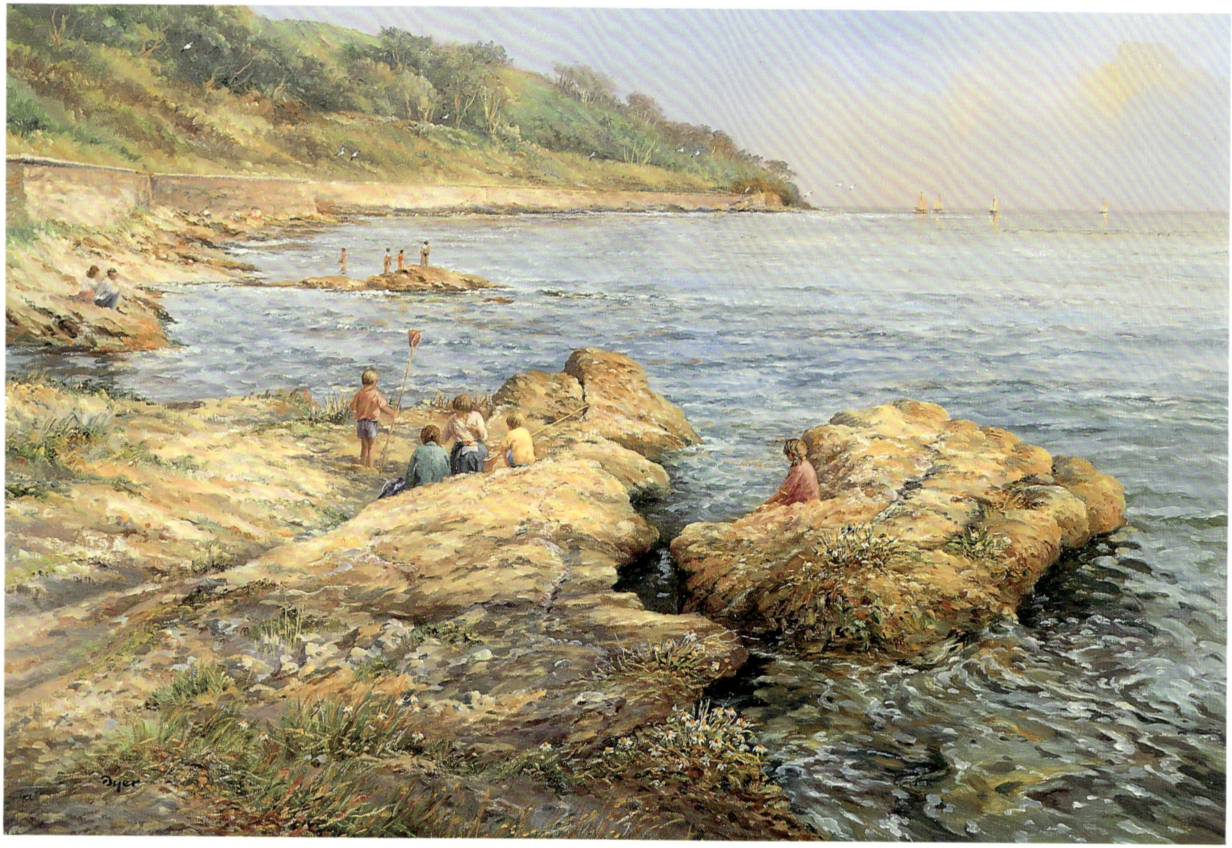

A Picnic on the Rocks, Castle Beach
20 x 30 inches, oil on canvas

Then there is Falmouth at play, with children picnicking and netting from the rocks at Castle Beach or in the transparent water towards Gyllyngvase. The bay is wide and from the far end the view extends to the entrance of Helford Creek and the Manacles beyond.

When the days are misty the sails hang at rest awaiting a breeze, with the town and tower looking on. In the first mist of autumn the colours change and the church, once almost hidden from above, stands quietly with the boats below.

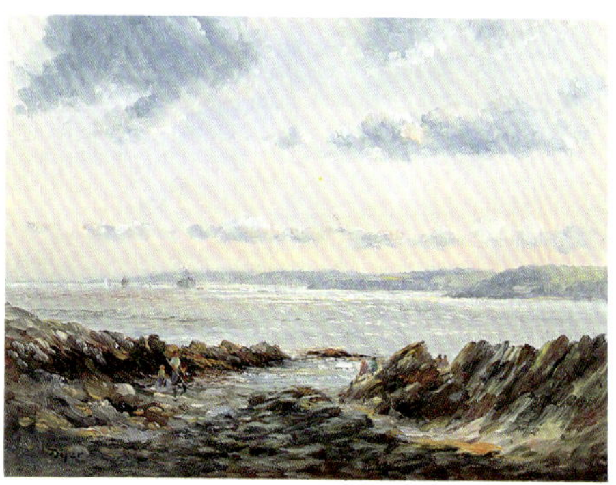

Sparkling Sea, Falmouth Bay
9 x 12 inches, oil sketch on board

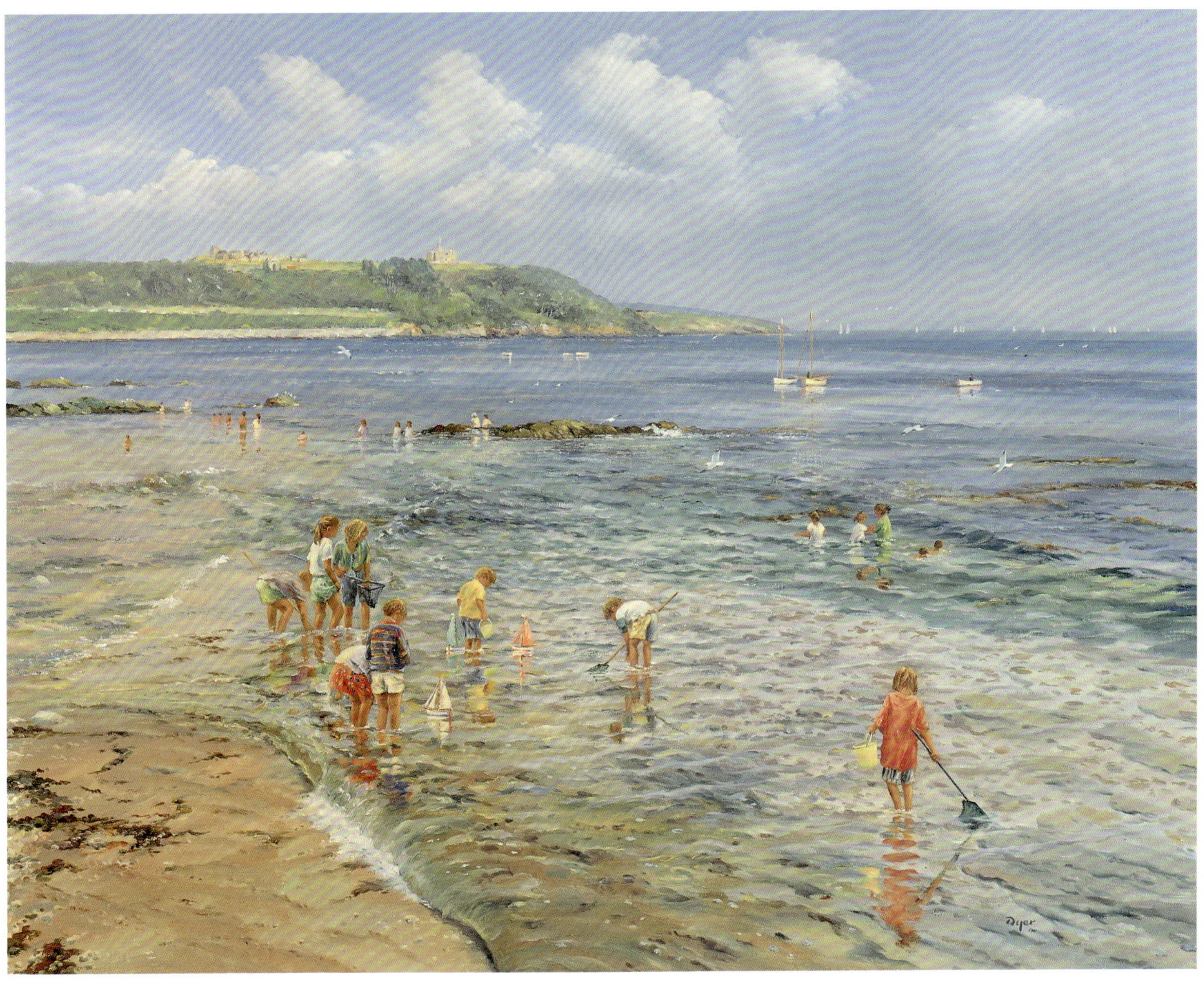

Clear Water, Castle Beach
28 x 36 inches, oil on canvas

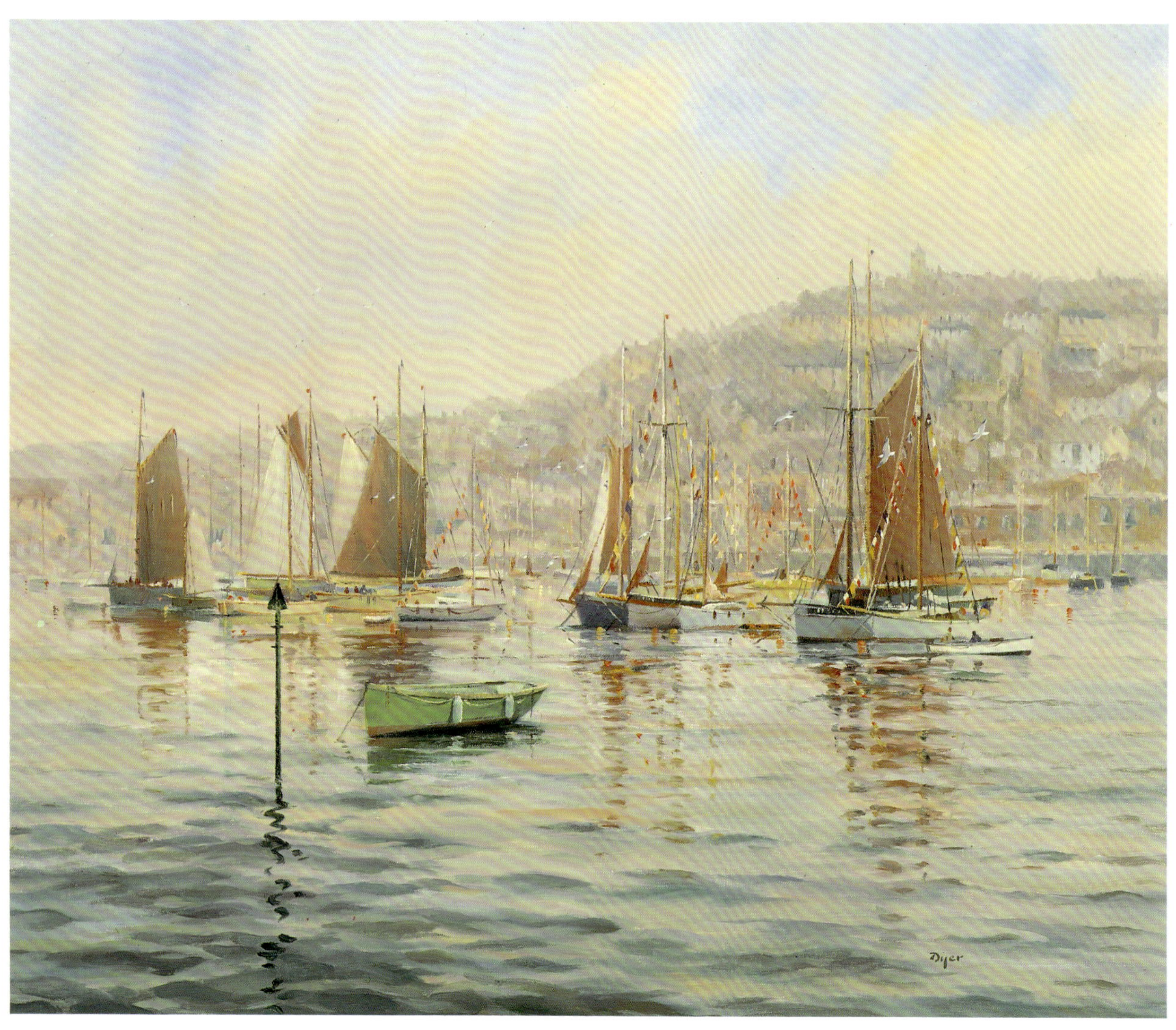

Misty Calm, Falmouth
20 x 24 inches, oil on canvas

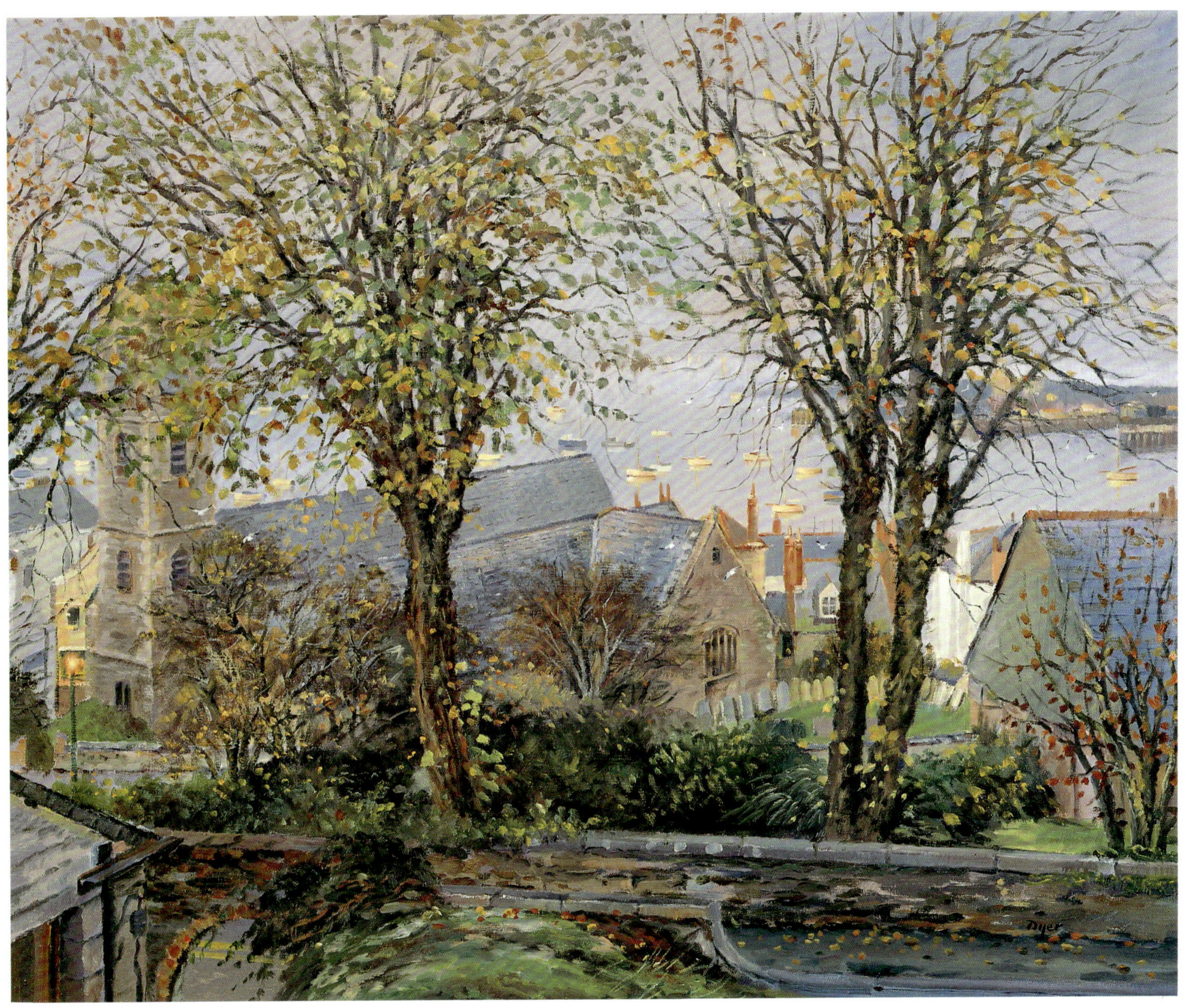

Autumn Trees above the Harbour, Falmouth
24 x 30 inches, oil on canvas

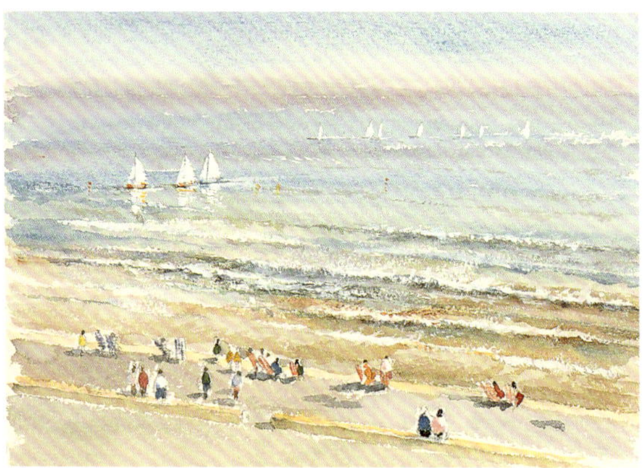

After the Race
7 x 10 inches, watercolour

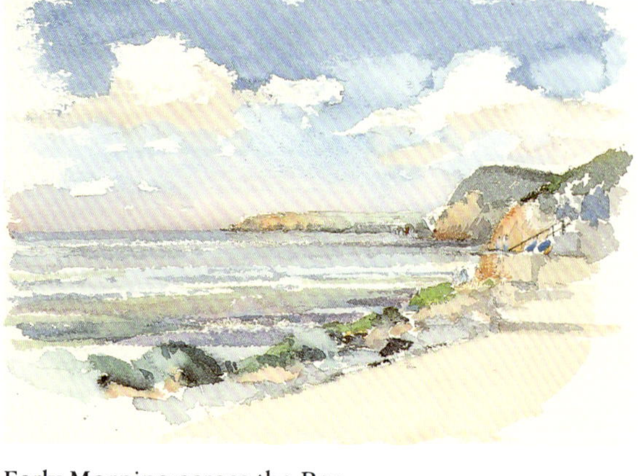

Early Morning across the Bay
7 x 10 inches, watercolour

Perhaps I should explain the means by which I work. Virtually all canvases are painted in my studio. My forays to the real world for source material are sometimes planned and sometimes spontaneous. This work includes photographs for reference, and sometimes on the spot oil sketches or watercolours. I do have to be careful that these sketches are not over finished as it can be embarrassing to say the least, when as happened at Priest's Cove, the local fishermen, whose seat I was using, went fishing, brought their catch back and drove it to Newlyn Market, only to return to find me still at work.

One day at Priest's Cove I managed to capture in an oil sketch the dramatic changing light and weather conditions across the Brisons. This sketch forms an important part of the Priest's Cove series culminating in the painting *"Fishing Boats at Priest's Cove"*.

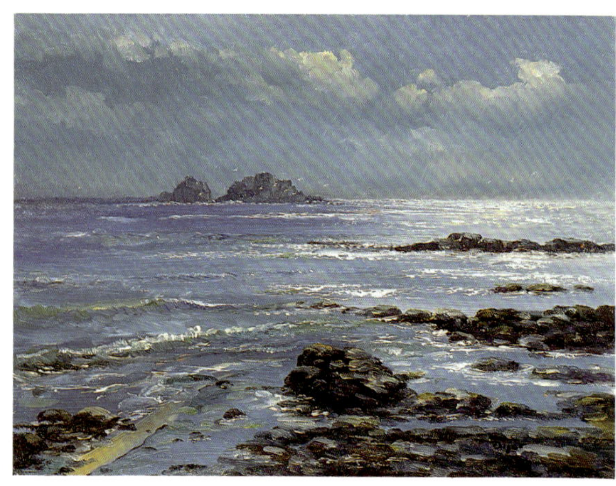

The Brisons from Priest's Cove
9 x 12 inches, oil sketch on board

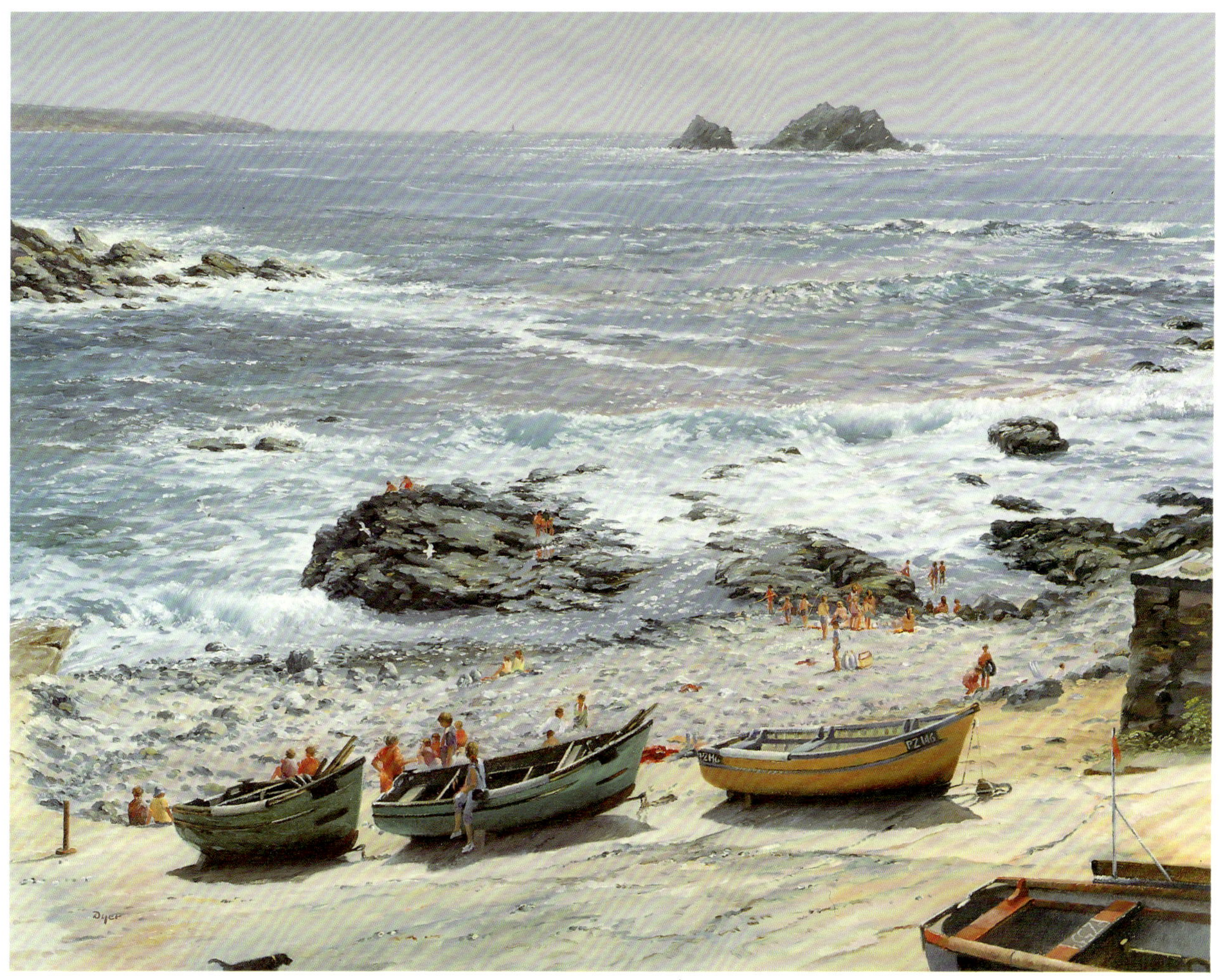

Fishing Boats at Priest's Cove
28 x 36 inches, oil on canvas

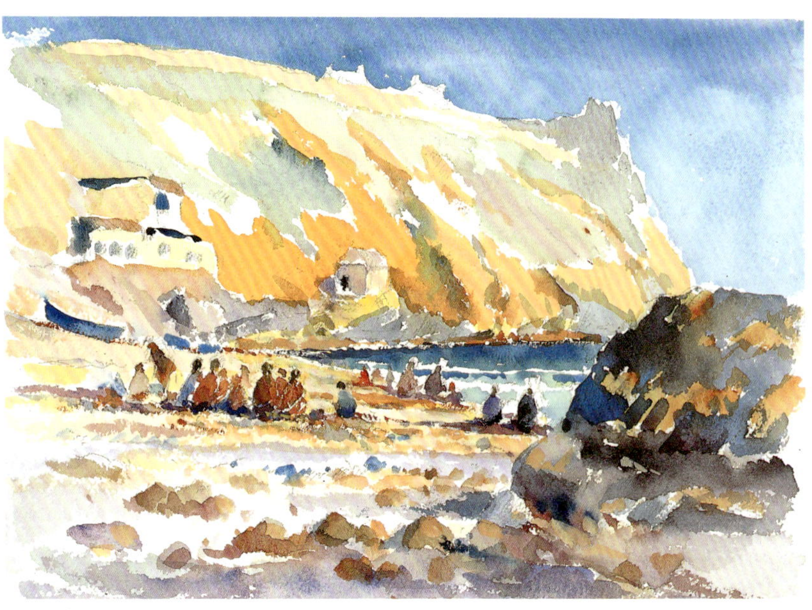

Evening at Priest's Cove, Cape Cornwall
9 x 12 inches, watercolour

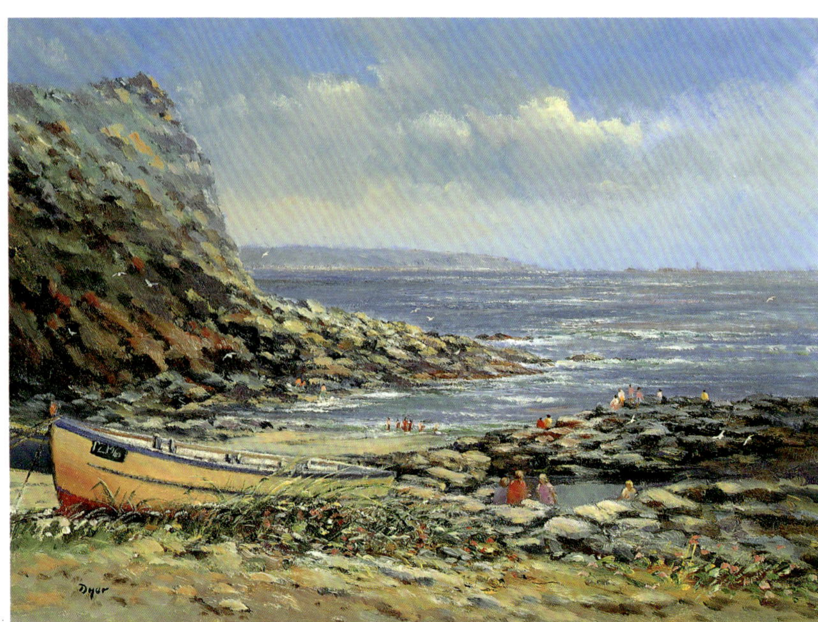

Looking towards the Longships from Priest's Cove
9 x 12 inches, oil sketch on board

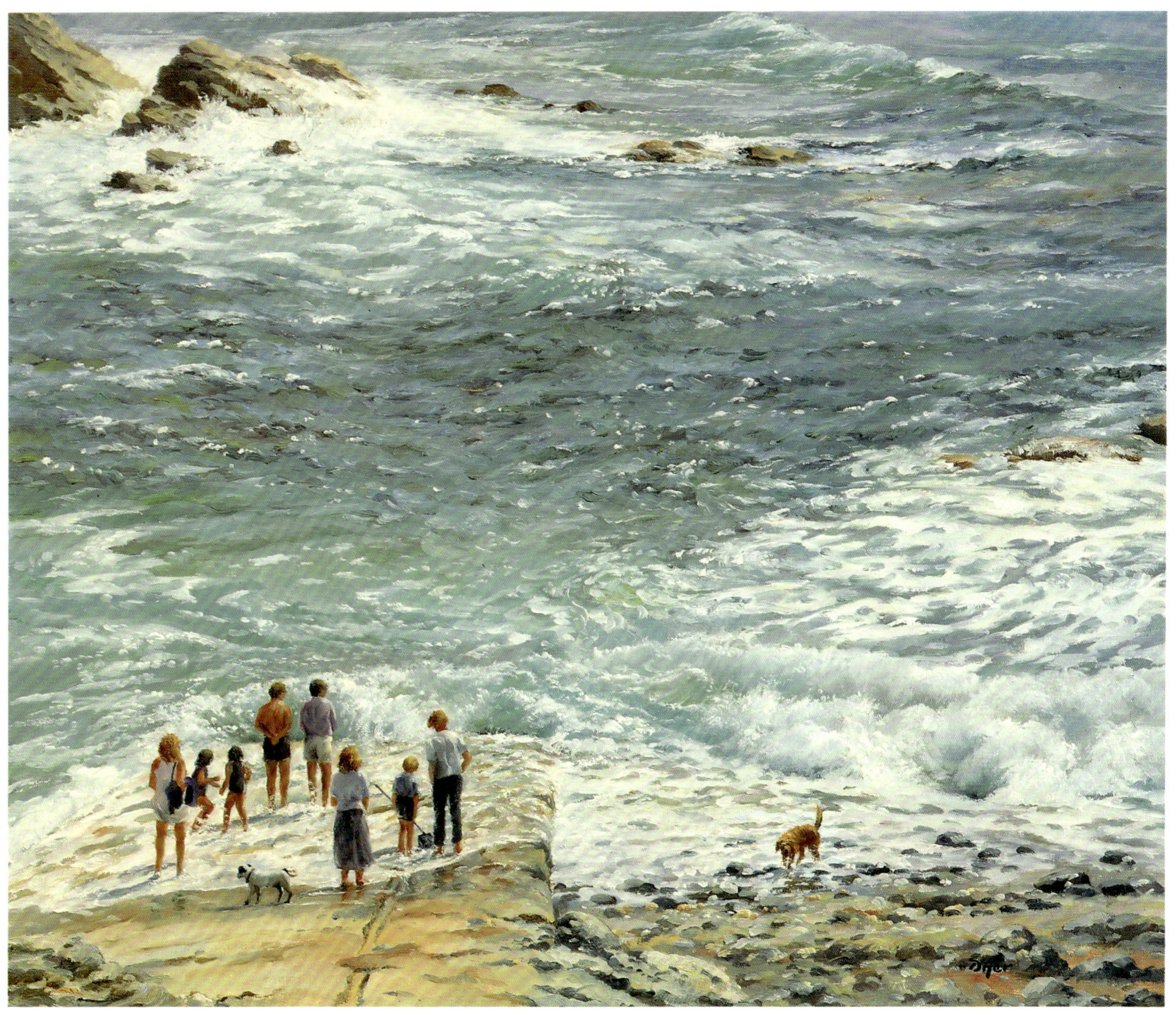

Watching the Waves, Priest's Cove
20 x 24 inches, oil on canvas

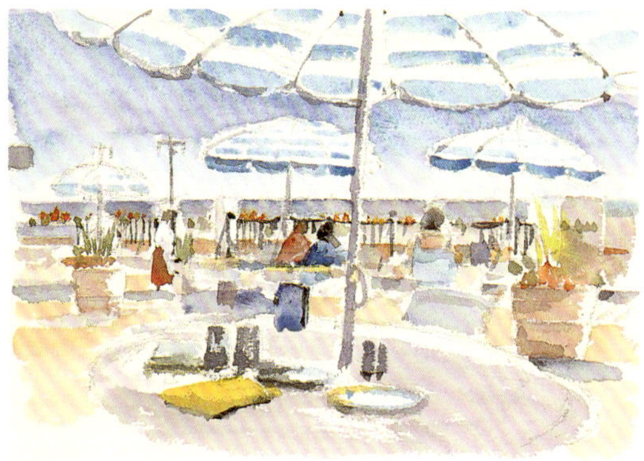

Blue Striped Umbrellas and Distant Sea
7 x 10 inches, watercolour

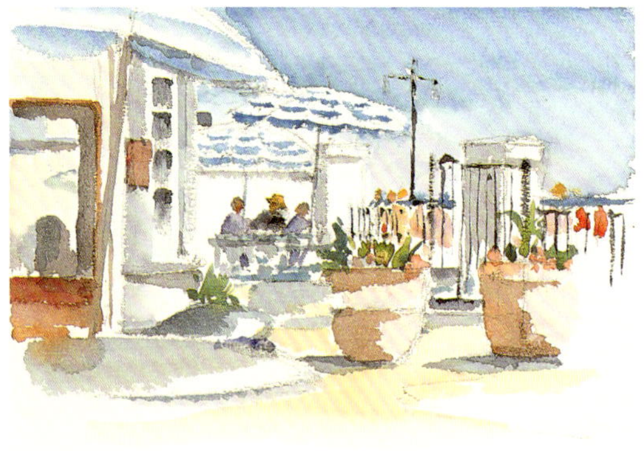

Sunshine on the Patio
7 x 10 inches, watercolour

Watercolours are a delight and a worry especially when working on the spot, whereas with oils the idea can be modified and altered to a degree (although with the risk of loosing freshness and spontaneity), watercolours need to be, well, just done, positively and clearly. One beautiful June day I had a very enjoyable time sitting on the seafront under blue striped umbrellas having coffee and lunch. This provided the ideal subject matter for a series of small watercolour paintings.

As a painter I constantly strive to capture the effect of light and shade which changes so quickly on the Cornish coast, it is the very act of the changing weather conditions that can so alter the mood of a place. On the South Coast of Cornwall at Rinsey, where the long Atlantic swell meets the land, I captured on canvas the foaming white breakers at the water's edge with the dark cliffs beyond. The colours in the shore are constantly enriched as the water glides over it, shining with reflective light. Children collect mother of pearl and limpet shells on the shoreline. In spring the cliffs are covered in pinks or thrift, and it is a delight to follow the small steep path to the hidden cove below.

In Springtime I love the early mornings with their freshness and 'ready for a new day' feeling. The sun warms the air on a May morning with the clouds reflecting the light above through the morning mist. Children eagerly get ready to fly their kites on the first sea breeze of the day. Although the air around the coastline is hardly ever still, sometimes the weather can change quickly and in less than half an hour the breeze may have vanished. If any of that small time span can be captured and held, what a prize it will be.

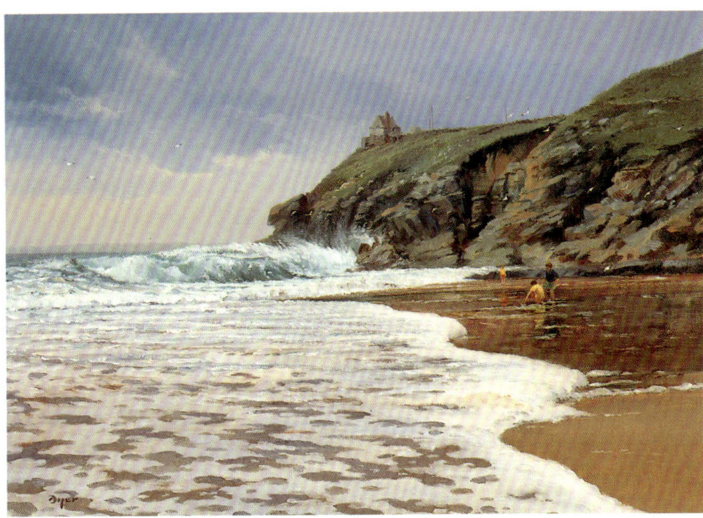

Towards Rinsey Headland from Porthcew Beach
10 x 14 inches, oil on canvas

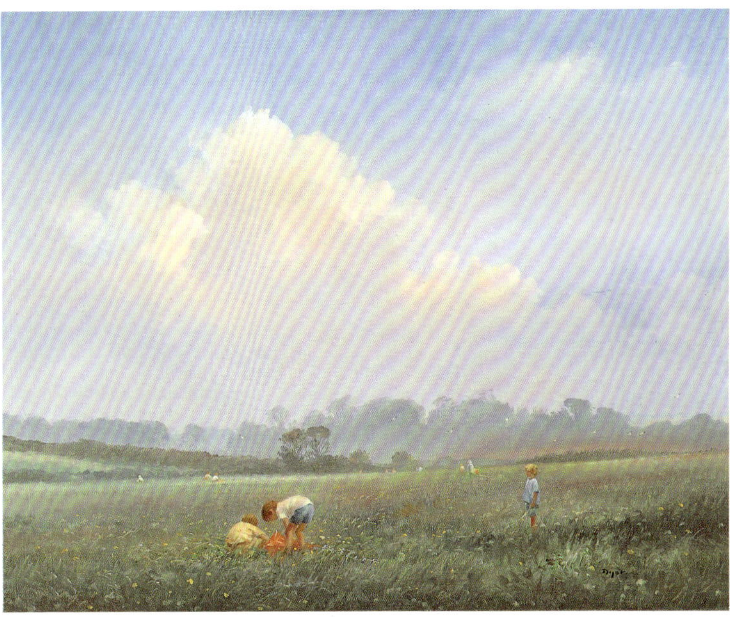

Early Morning Kite Flying
16 x 20 inches, oil on canvas

LET ME relate my first real encounter with Polwheveral Creek. I always thought there was no access to it except for the owners of private properties, but one day as I was driving through I spotted an elderly lady by a cottage, and pulling over I asked her whether it would be possible to walk to the creek a little way below. "Of course" she said. There was a way alongside her property. So through the gate I went, John my son with me. On the way through the gate I noticed that where the throw over hook was bent over its anchor point the metal had worn away to a smooth and thin diameter and that it was now no more than a thick thread, although still intact. She had been born there, lived all her life there and was quite content. We closed the gate carefully, thanking her, and arrived at the head of the creek.

The heat was almost unbearable; the humidity certainly was. I half expected the partly sunken branches of trees to show themselves as crocodiles or to see parrots flying through the trees. Instead of which there was the sound of running water and slurpy gurgling noises from the creek and in the shallows I could see small fish enjoying the warmth of the primeval mud. Further in the distance there was a heron and out in the deeper water fish could be heard jumping.

Looking towards the seaward end of Polwheveral the banks on either side have a different character. To the right, fields sweep down to the trees at the edge of the creek forming good picnic spots. On the left bank there are small beach-like areas, normally covered at a high tide. At the head of the creek there are springy but water filled grass tufts where small moored boats can be seen resting in the muddy channel to the part where the branches of oak trees sweep downward. These are not the dwarf trees of most Cornish creeks but really handsome specimens.

Continuing along the creek small abandoned jetties can be found, from a time long ago when ore was the coinage of the day. The foreshore here is shingly and shell like. Looking back at the cottages they seem enclosed in a different world compared to the slightly widening area of water immediately ahead. How still, as if nothing will ever change.

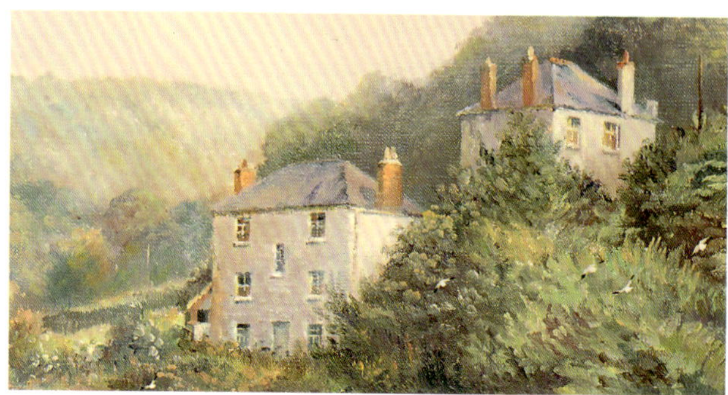

Returning to Polwheveral in the autumn can be a delight, for if the summer has been good and the winds light and rain has not made the air heavy with lingering wetness, then the oaks are splendid. Rusty yellow and dull red coats reflected in still waters. Then there are the unexpected but fairly constant deep plops. You really need a safety helmet to walk under them for I have never seen or heard such an abundance of acorns. One might expect to see colonies of squirrels above and herds of pigs eager to rummage below.

Then last spring, I heard that the lady who had shown us the way had passed on and I noticed on my next visit that the metal of the throw over hook on the gate had finally parted. I wondered if the two were of the same good age, from a time when a fastening and a way of life were good enough not even to think about changing.

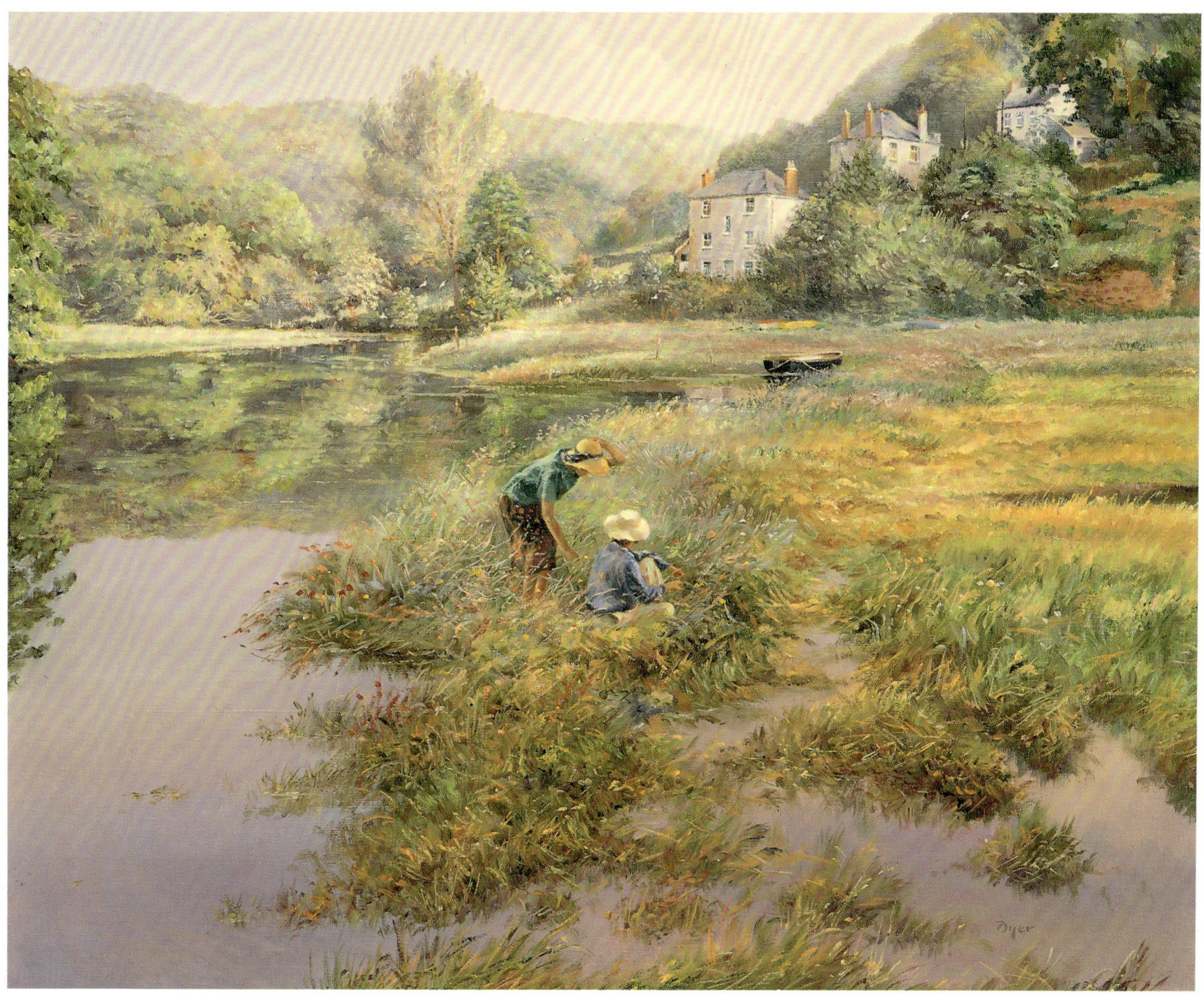

High Tide on a Glorious Day
24 x 30 inches, oil on canvas

Left: Detail of, High Tide on a Glorious Day

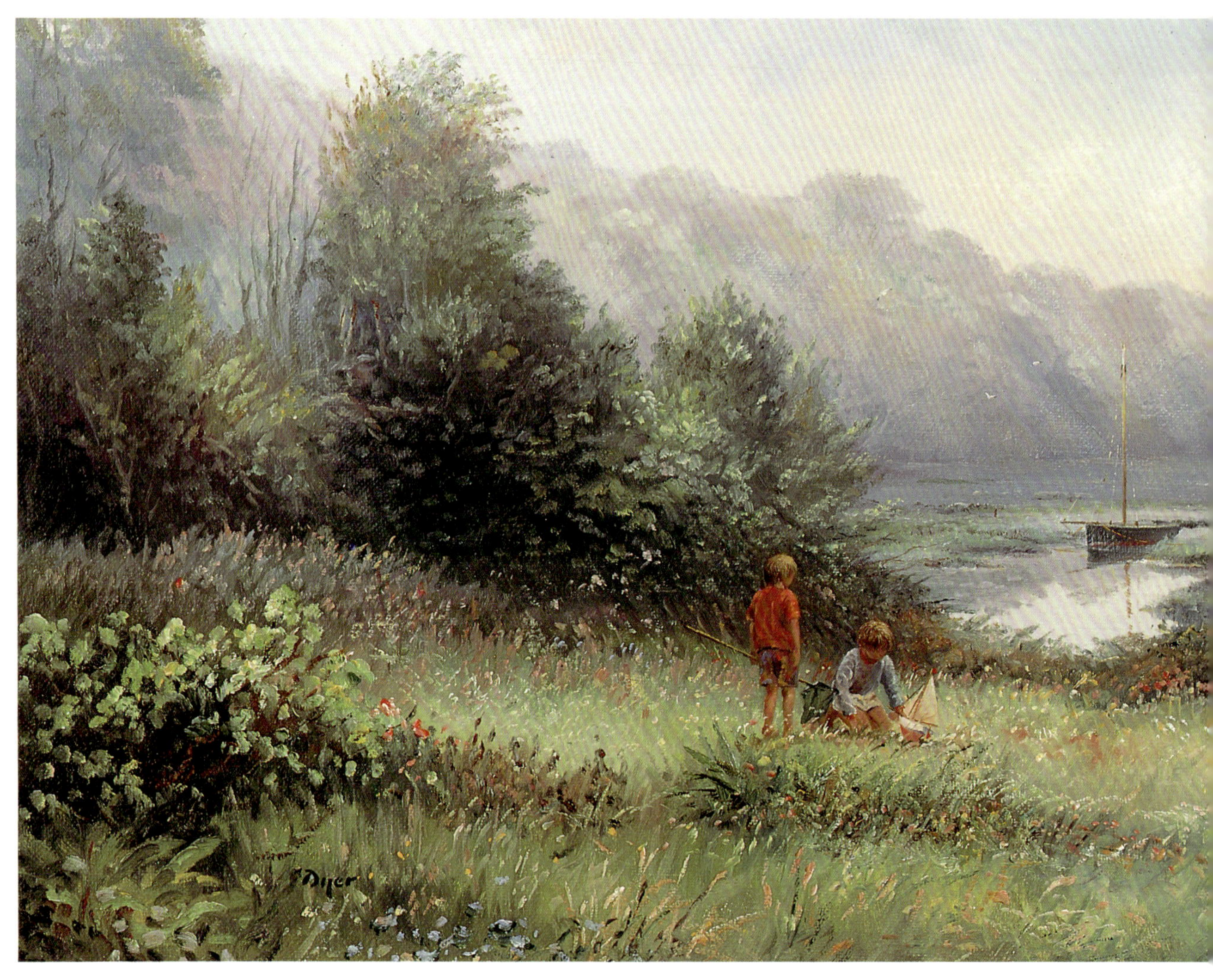

Early Morning View across Polwheveral Creek
18 x 48 inches, oil on canvas

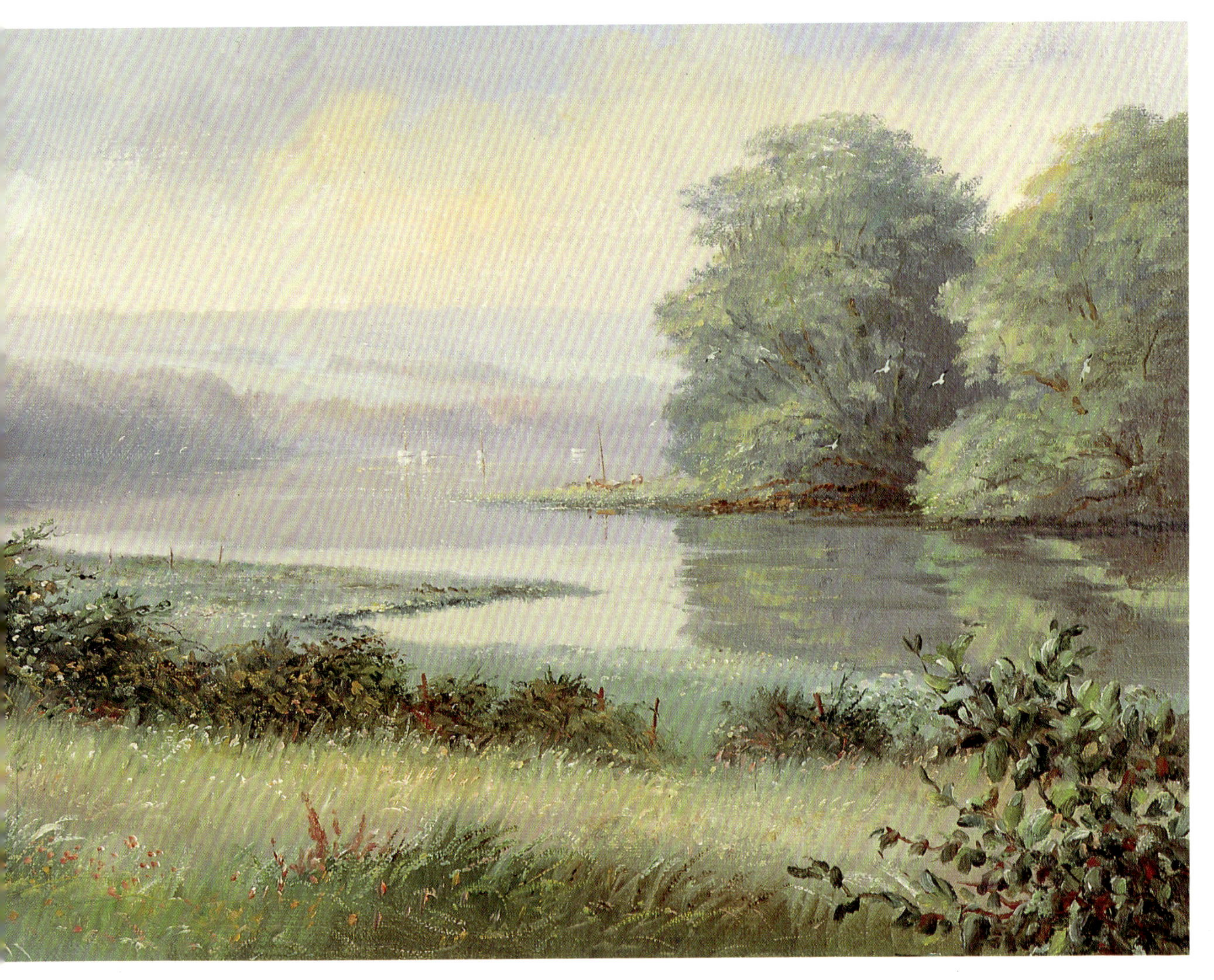

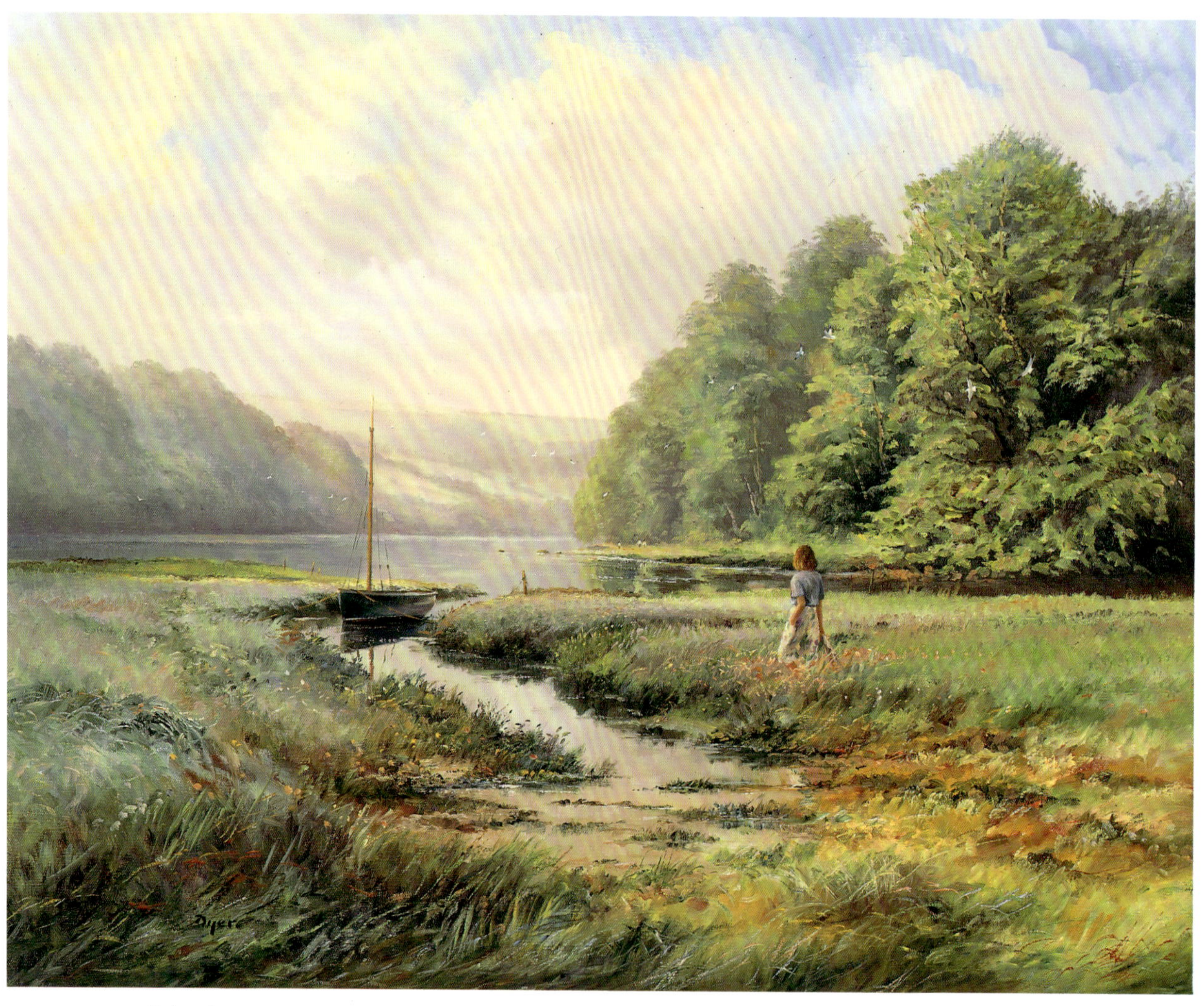

A Morning Walk by the Quiet Waters, Polwheveral
24 x 30 inches, oil on canvas

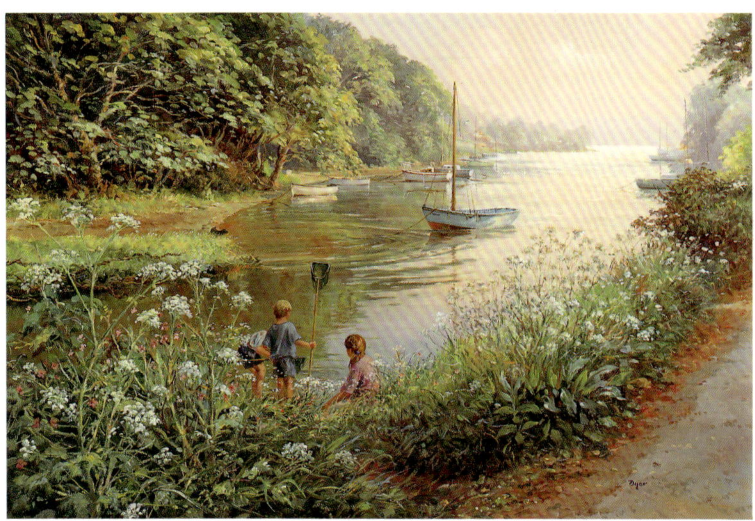

Evening Porth Navas Creek
20 x 30 inches, oil on canvas

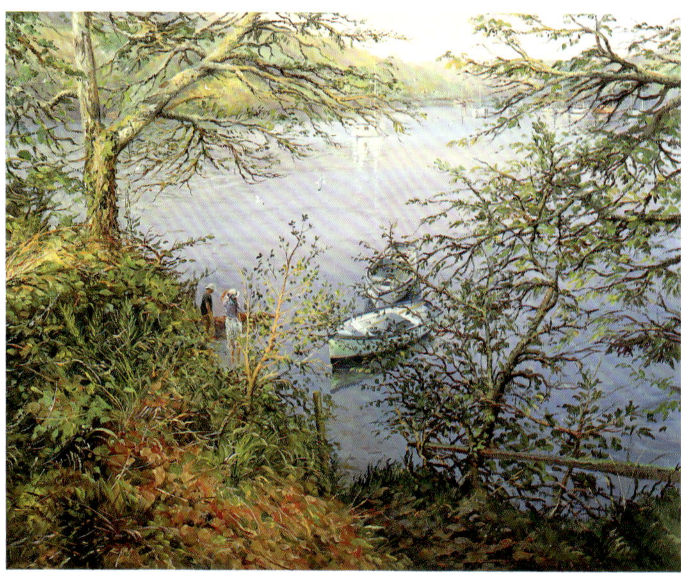

Blue Water through the Trees, Coombe
24 x 30 inches, oil on canvas

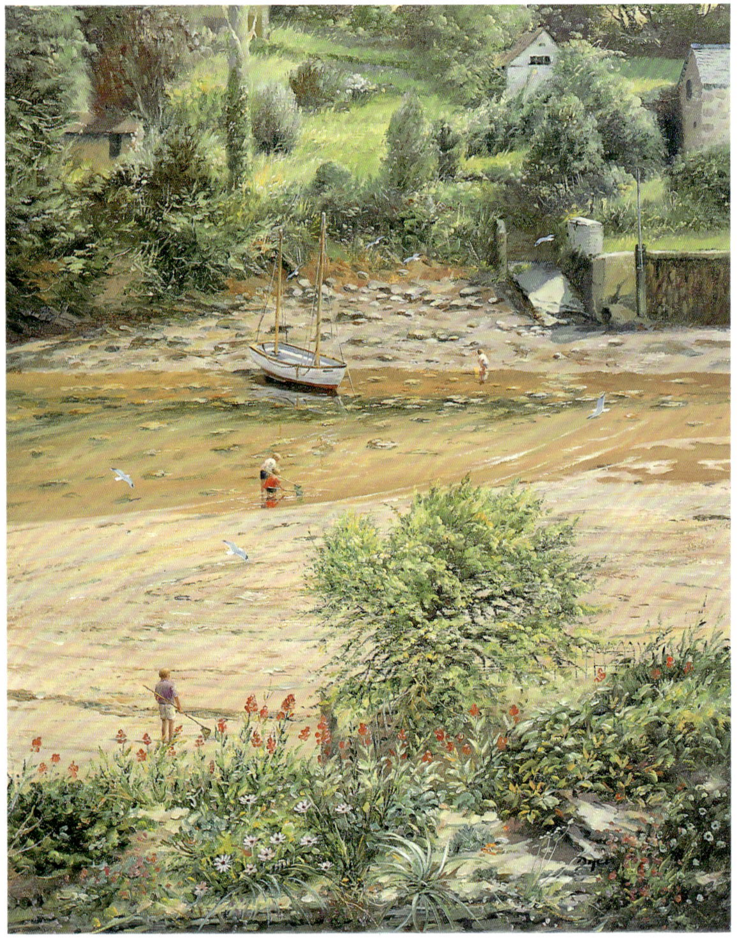

Shallow Waters, Helford
24 x 20 inches, oil on canvas

Right: Springtime at Helford
28 x 36 inches, oil on canvas

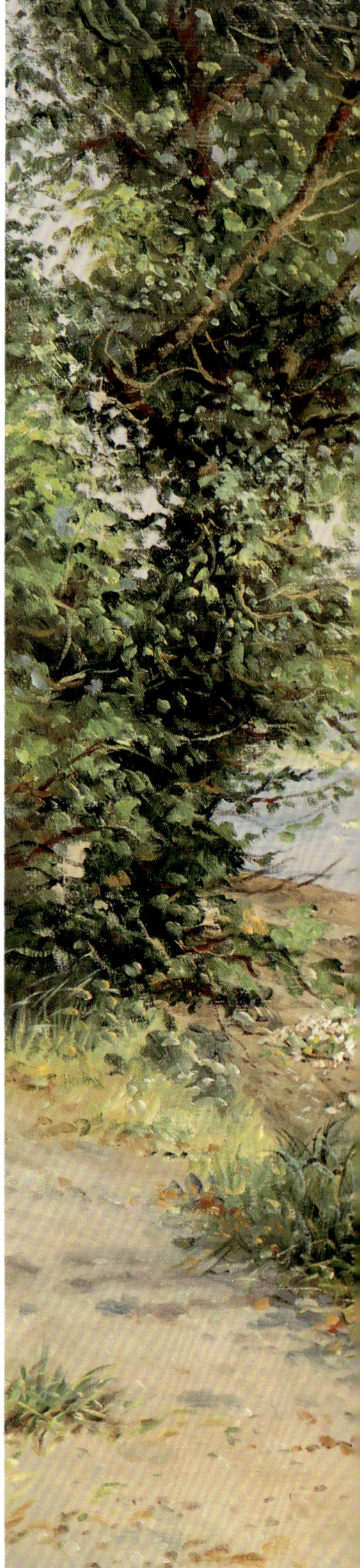

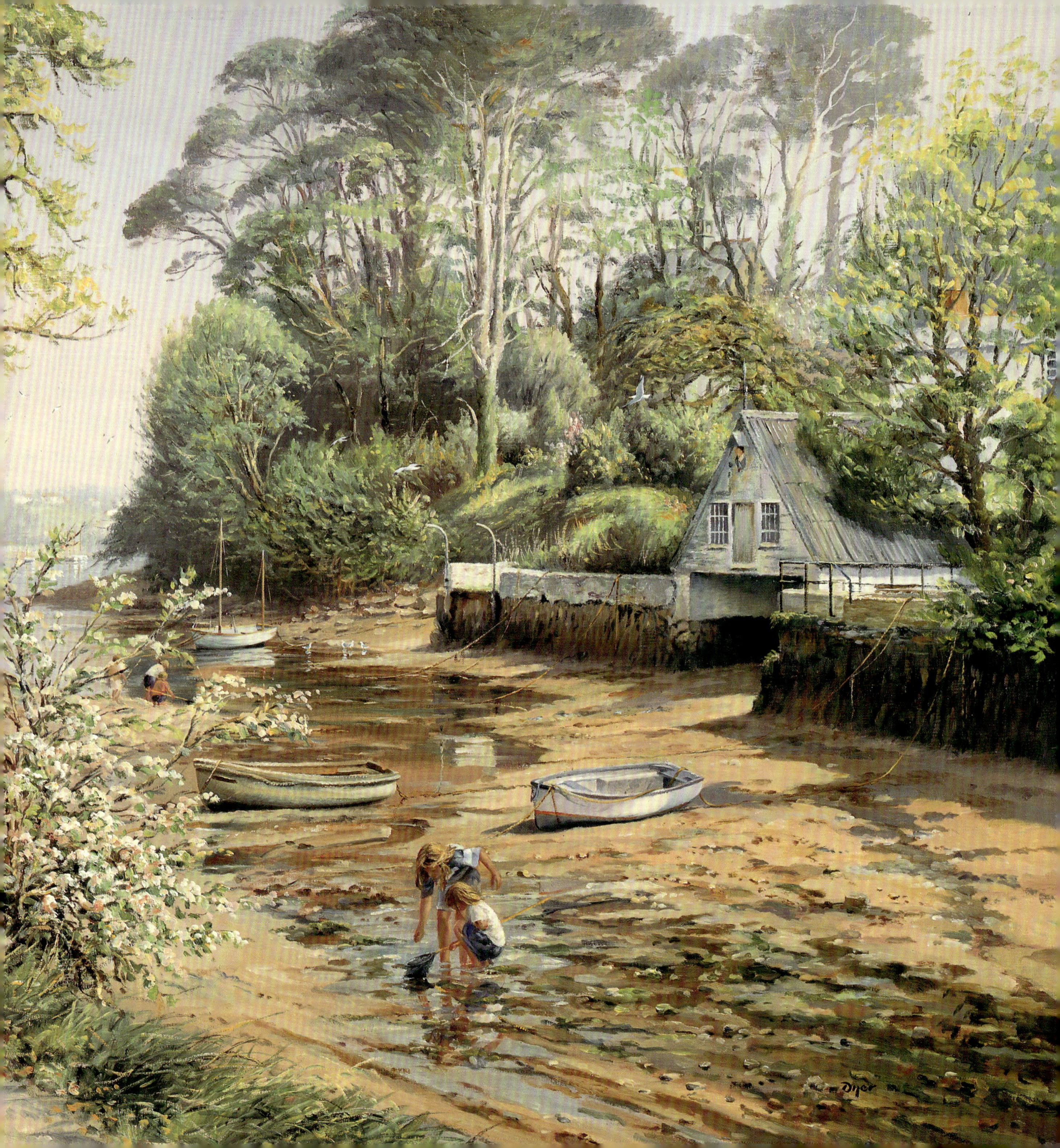
Dyer

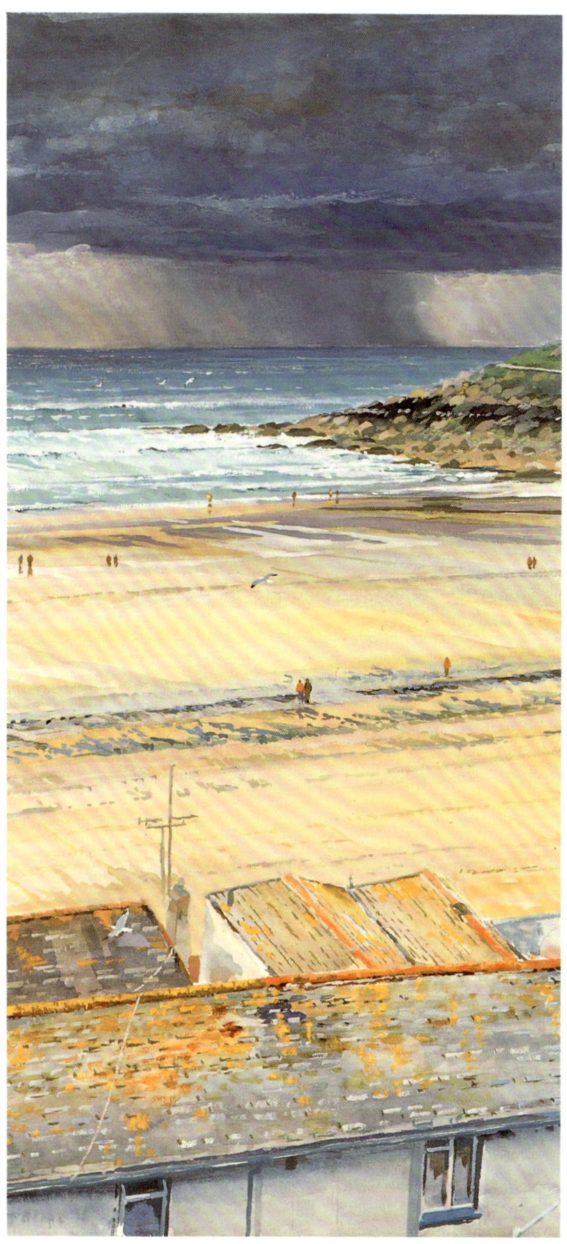

Detail of, Rain Clouds over Porthmeor beach
22 x 22 inches, watercolour

From St. Ives on the North Coast of Cornwall one can see Hayle, the white lighthouse at Godrevy, and further on Cligga Head; a wild disused mining spot where winter waves crash in and the cliffs are spotted with adit holes. Back along the coast is the tiny beach at Chapel Porth, with transparent waves which push the holiday makers back and back.

To return to St. Ives. The beaches seem to glow and in daylight, I am told, it is the reflective qualities of the quartz which gives such luminescence. St. Ives bathed in its own light and now with a national figurehead, a splendidly white and proud building, The Tate of the West, which overlooks Porthmeor beach, with Clodgy Point one way and The Island the other.

On the harbour side the sand is rich and dense to the touch. At low tide outside the harbour wall pools are formed, perfect for exploring with bucket and net. On an ideal day small waves break with a depth and intensity of colour that ranges from light blue green to a tropical storm of indigo and ultramarine. In the distance stands Godrevy Lighthouse, a warning to sailors of past and present, giving the appearance of having its back to the sea owing to its position on the island it was built on. Today though, all is high summer colour, people relaxing and having fun. Sail the boats, fish the pools, swim, swim, swim. A memory of such a day will refresh for life.

Then evening with patches of light across the beach. Most families have either gone home or are having their evening meal. One or two though by the waters edge are still playing on the sand. Perhaps the best part of the day, with memories stored and safe and the day's magic lingers for a little time yet. Summer days are long, and the best of them warm and still as well.

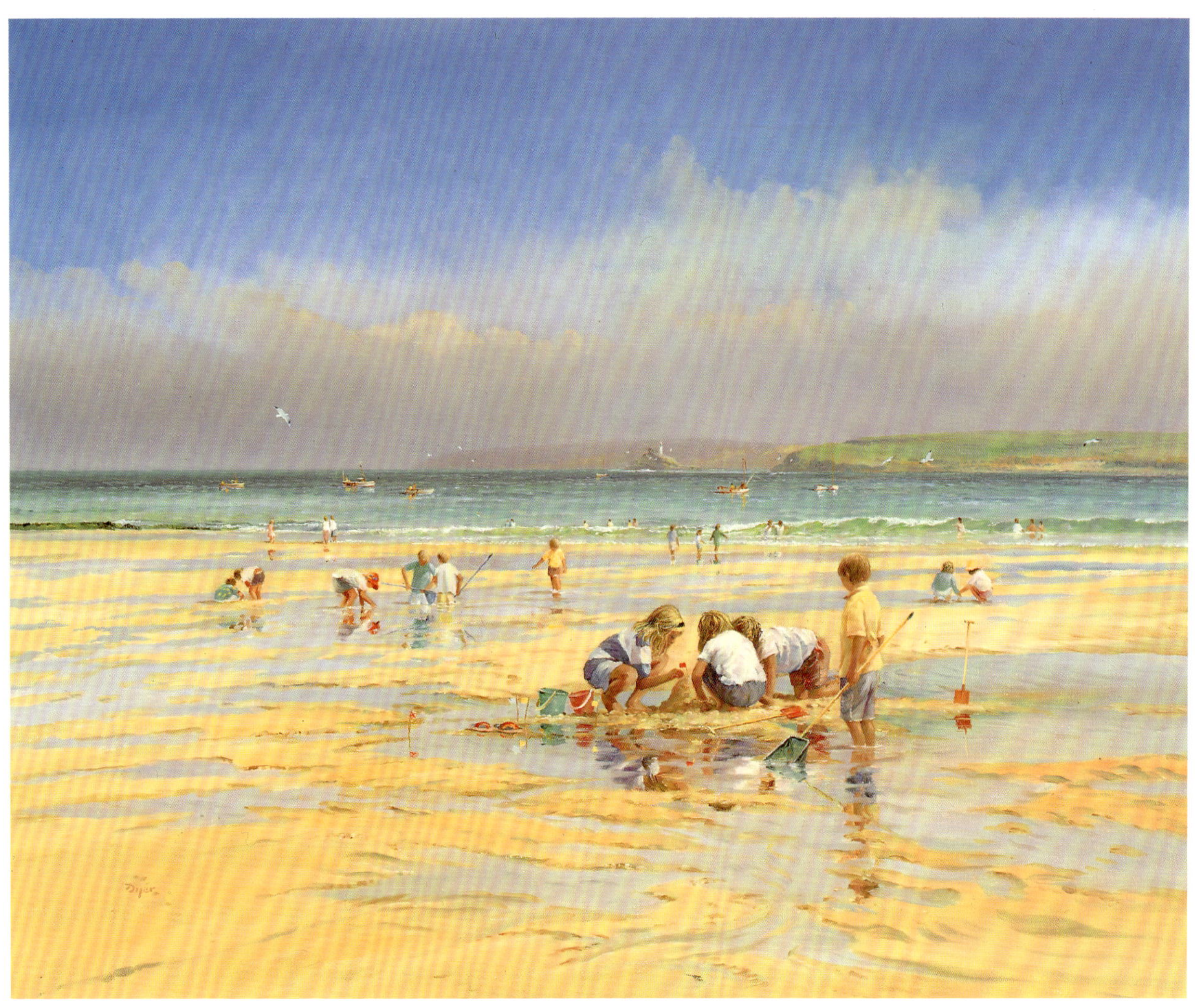

Summer Days, St. Ives
24 x 30 inches, oil on canvas

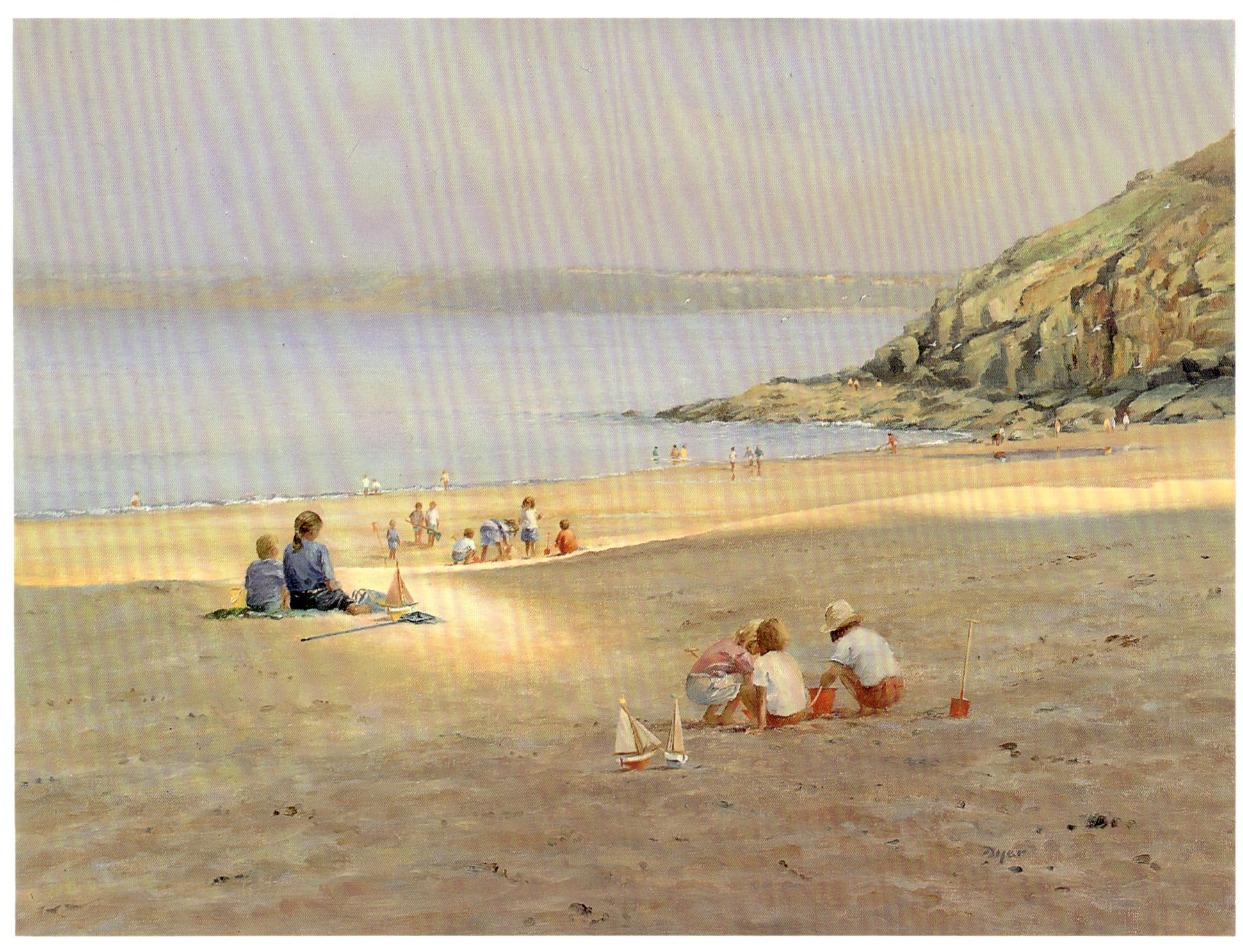

Evening Shadows, Porthminster Beach
16 x 22 inches, oil on canvas

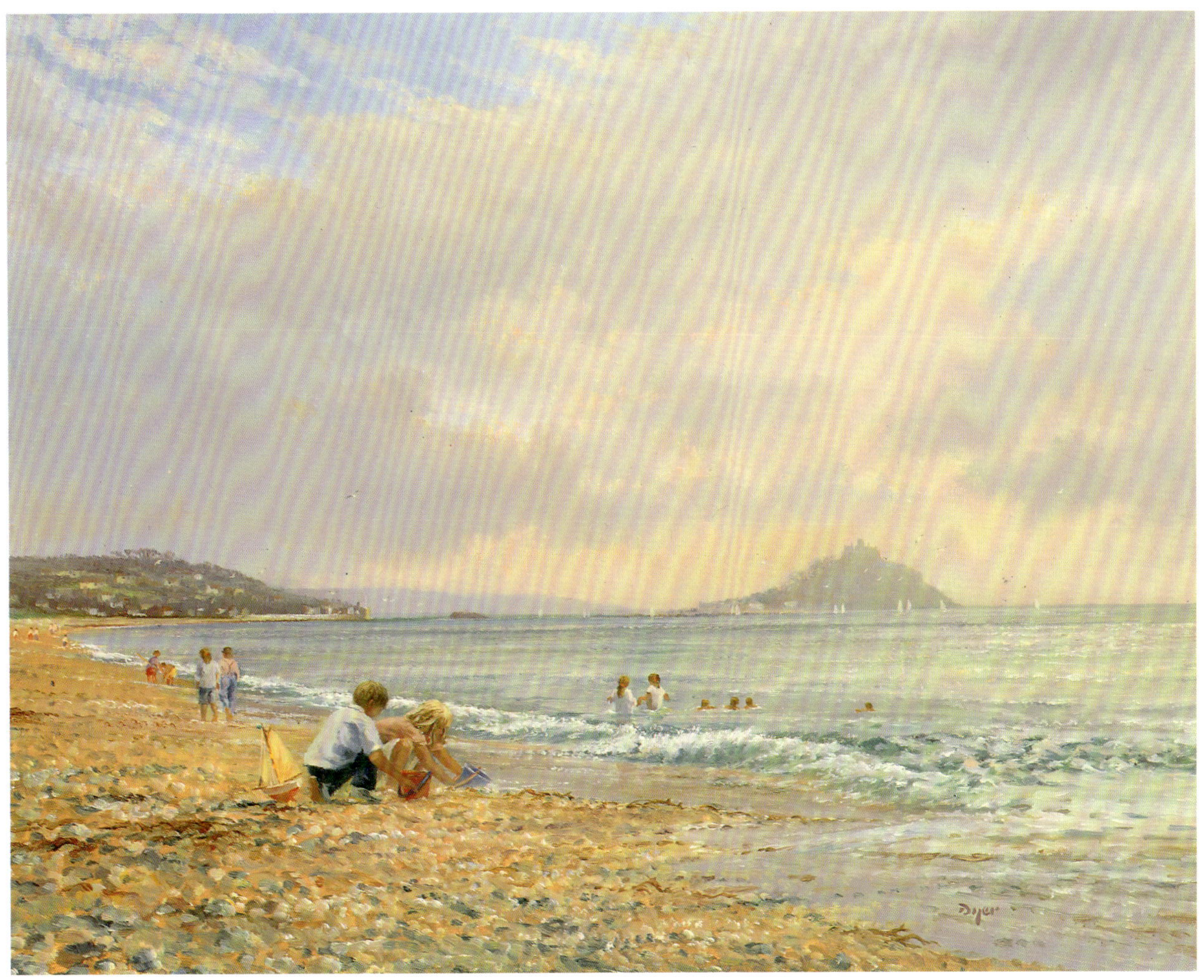

At the Water's Edge, Mounts Bay
16 x 20 inches, oil on canvas

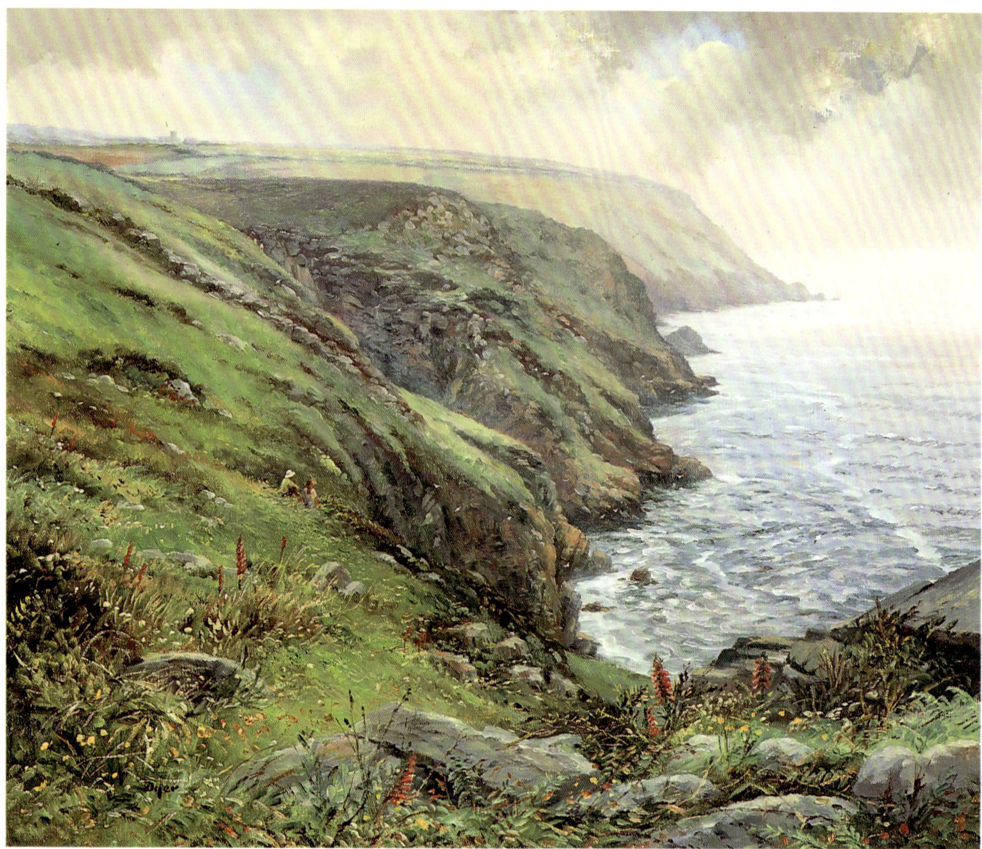

Springtime Path to Morvah
20 x 24 inches, oil on canvas

The road from St. Ives to St. Just is I think one of the finest coastal roads anywhere. This road which is really only a modernised tarmac farm track takes you past medieval farm fields and barren outcrops of rock. From here glimpses of coves can be seen with the cliff top Church at Morvah, St. Senara's Church at Zennor and Botallack further down the coast.

In early summer there are foxgloves, campion and wild grasses covering the cliffs and just off the road, silence. Not the town dweller's silence, but the quietness of undisturbed, unhumanised nature. It isn't a vacuum of course, there is the ever present sea and the soft swishing of the grass and foliage in the almost ever present wind. Sounds can be heard from afar; the distant call of a farm dog or a cry from a gull below. There is great depth and quality to the sounds which hang in the air, undisturbed, for a very long time.

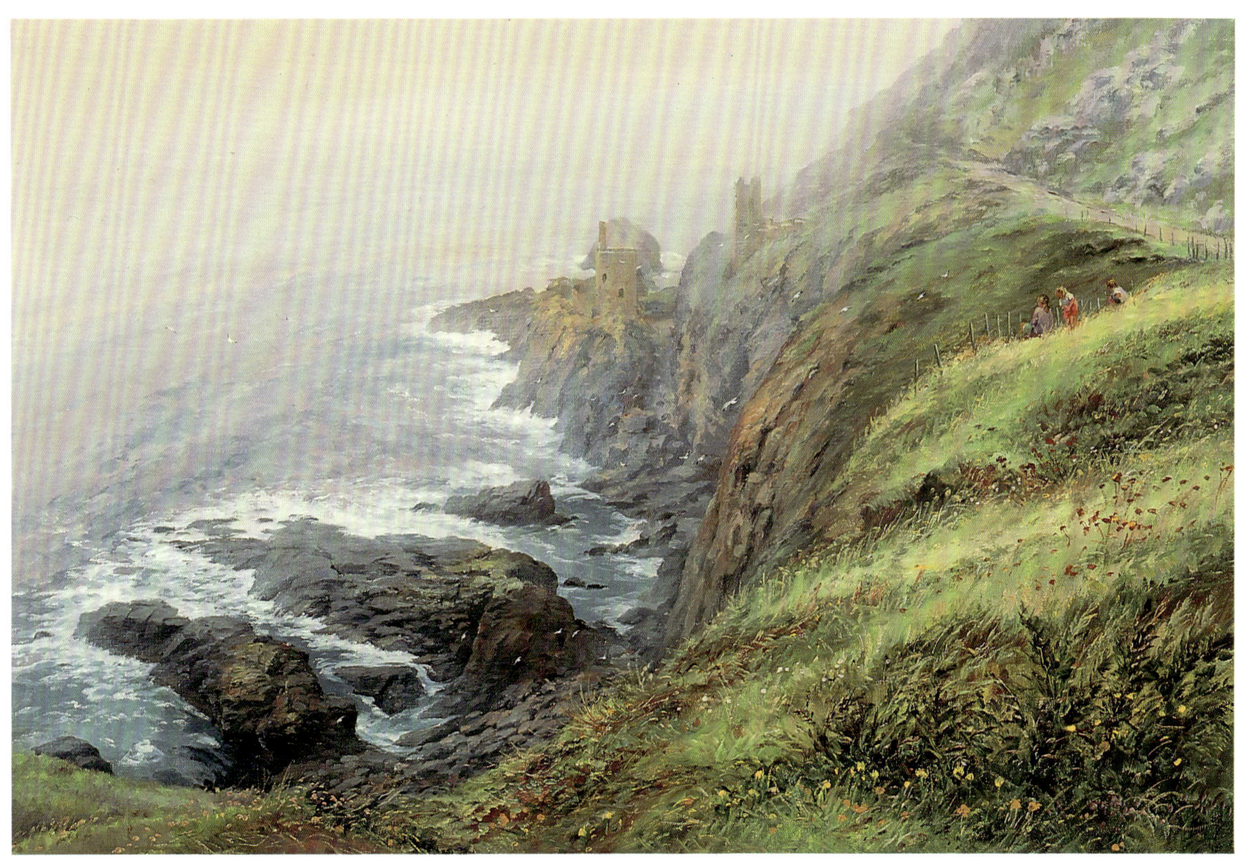

Mist over The Crowns, Botallack
20 x 30 inches, oil on canvas

Then the weather will change, and sometimes very quickly. But the effect is always worth watching, for it is because this part of Cornwall spearheads straight towards the Atlantic that changes are sometimes so dramatic.

The area around Botallack is one that is rich in mine workings with the deepest levels running far out under the sea. It is an isolated area often shrouded in mist with a uniquely Cornish atmosphere. The landscape is spectacular with a mixture of flower covered cliffs above and old engine houses (The Crowns) below. These are the remains of an industry which has now almost vanished, with the engine houses standing in harmony with the rugged coastal surroundings. So here man and nature have formed a sort of union much in the way that the fishermen with their small boats have in the small exposed coves.

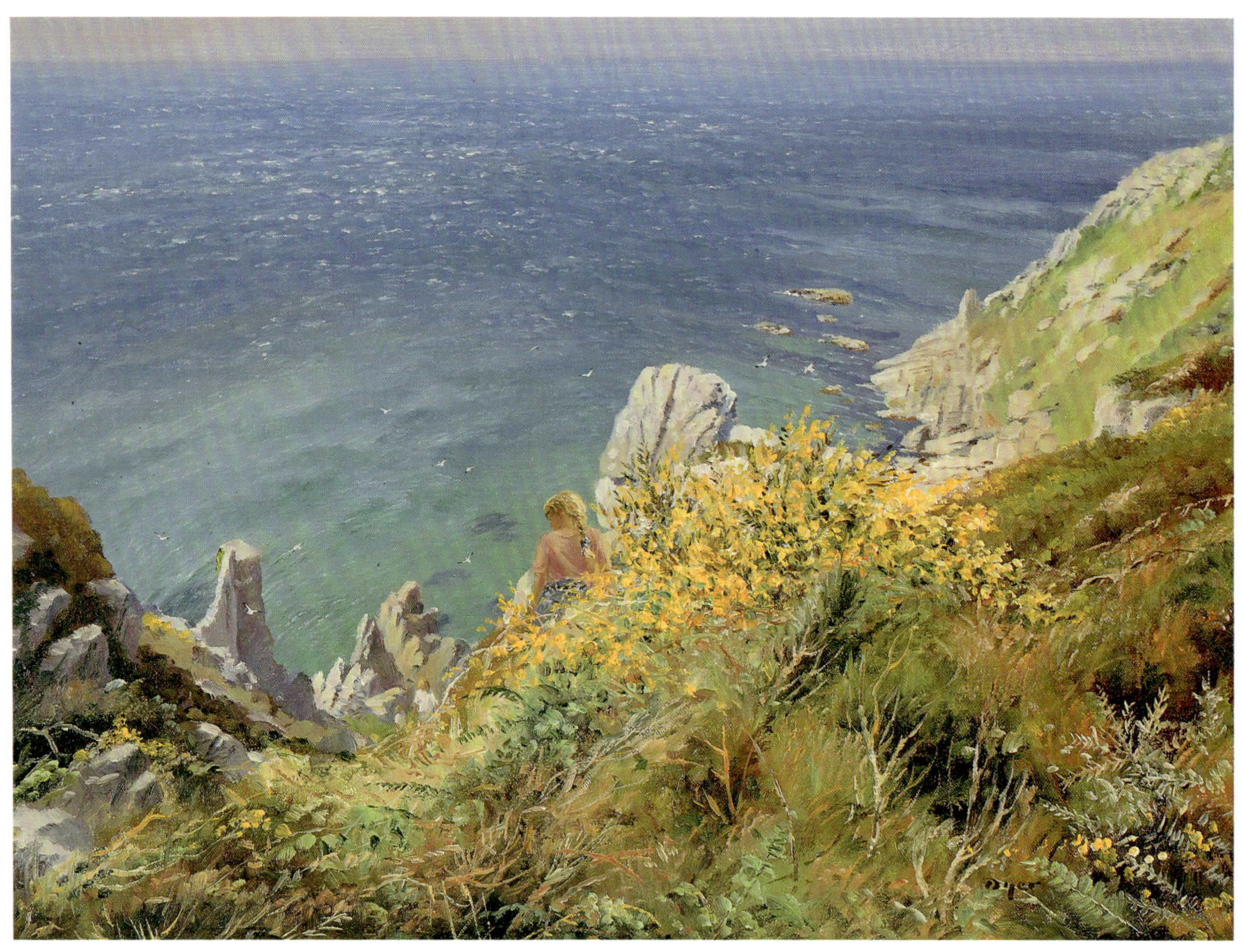

Turquoise Sea and Golden Gorse, Rosemergy
12 x 16 inches, oil on canvas

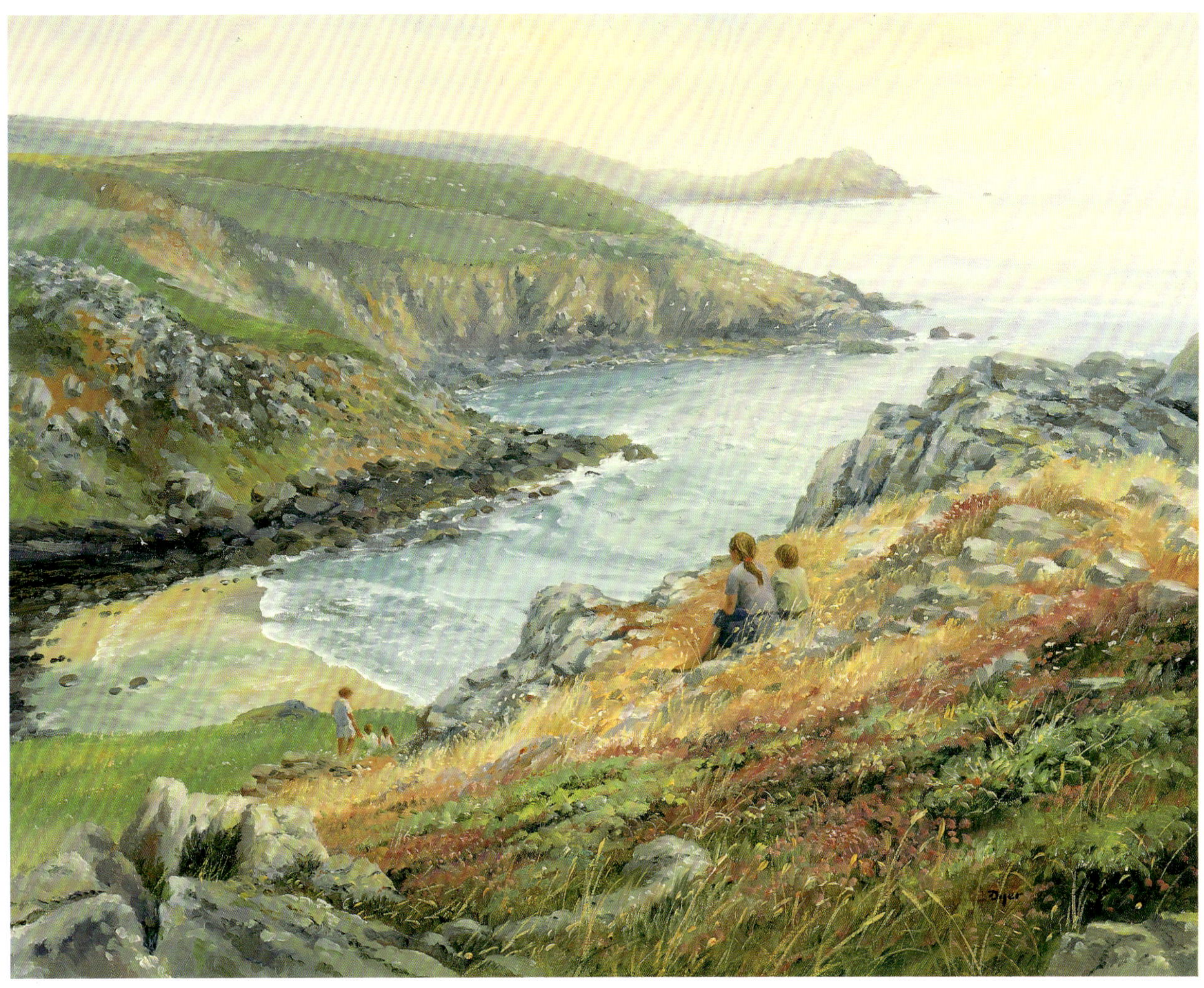

Purple Heather on the Cliffs, Mermaid's Cove
24 x 30 inches, oil on canvas

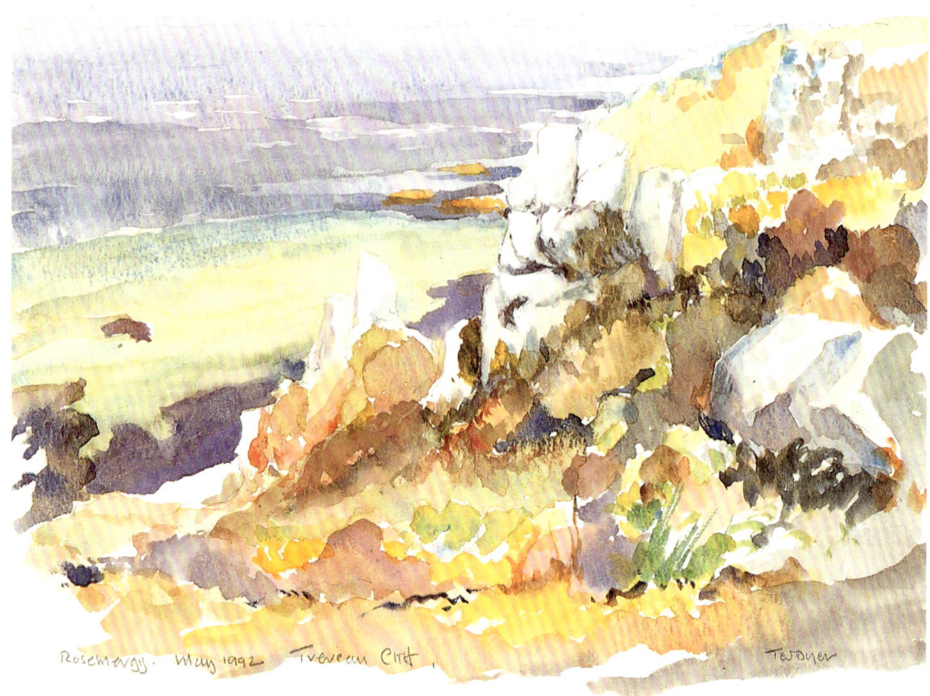

A Bright Day at Rosemergy
9 x 11.5 inches, watercolour

I have painted around and from the headland of Zennor with the Mermaid's Cove below and the sea a clear tranquil green. Also the stream which finds its way eventually to the beach over rocks and forming pools on the way. I wonder if the legend is true about the mermaid who lured a chorister down this watery way to the sea at Pendour Cove below. If it is true then on a warm summer evening the lovers can still be heard singing together at Pendour or as it is known locally, Mermaid's Cove. I somehow hope it is, if not it should be.

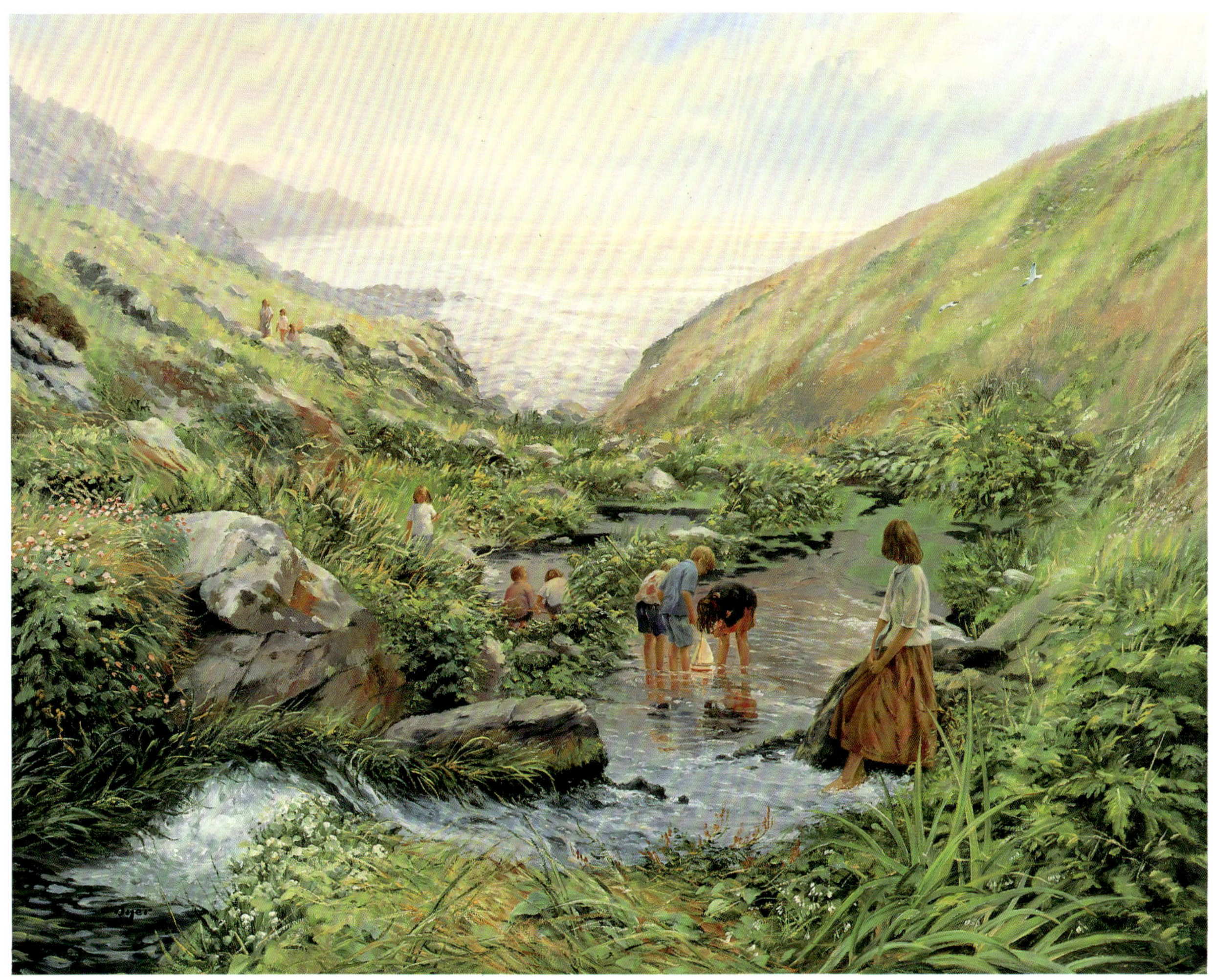

Playing in the Pool above Mermaid's Cove, Zennor
28 x 36 inches, oil on canvas

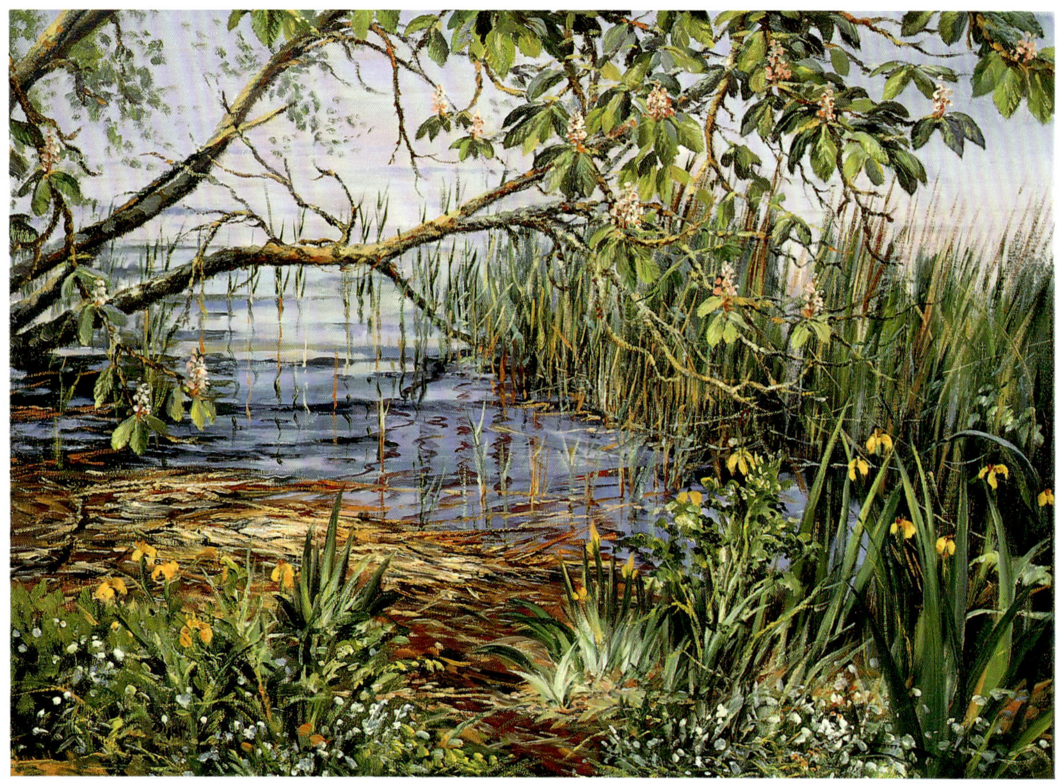

Horse Chestnut and Wild Iris
16 x 22 inches, oil on canvas

Wild flowers are so much part of Cornwall that I had to include the wild iris reflected in their watery setting and the horse chestnut reaching down to them, and later in the year hydrangeas bathed in soft light with Helford Creek in the distance. Also the South Coast near Port Loe has marvellously spiky blackthorn and gorse which I came across one spring day, and further east towards Mevagissey, where the countryside changes character slightly with long sloping fields of buttercups which sweep downward to the tranquil sea below.

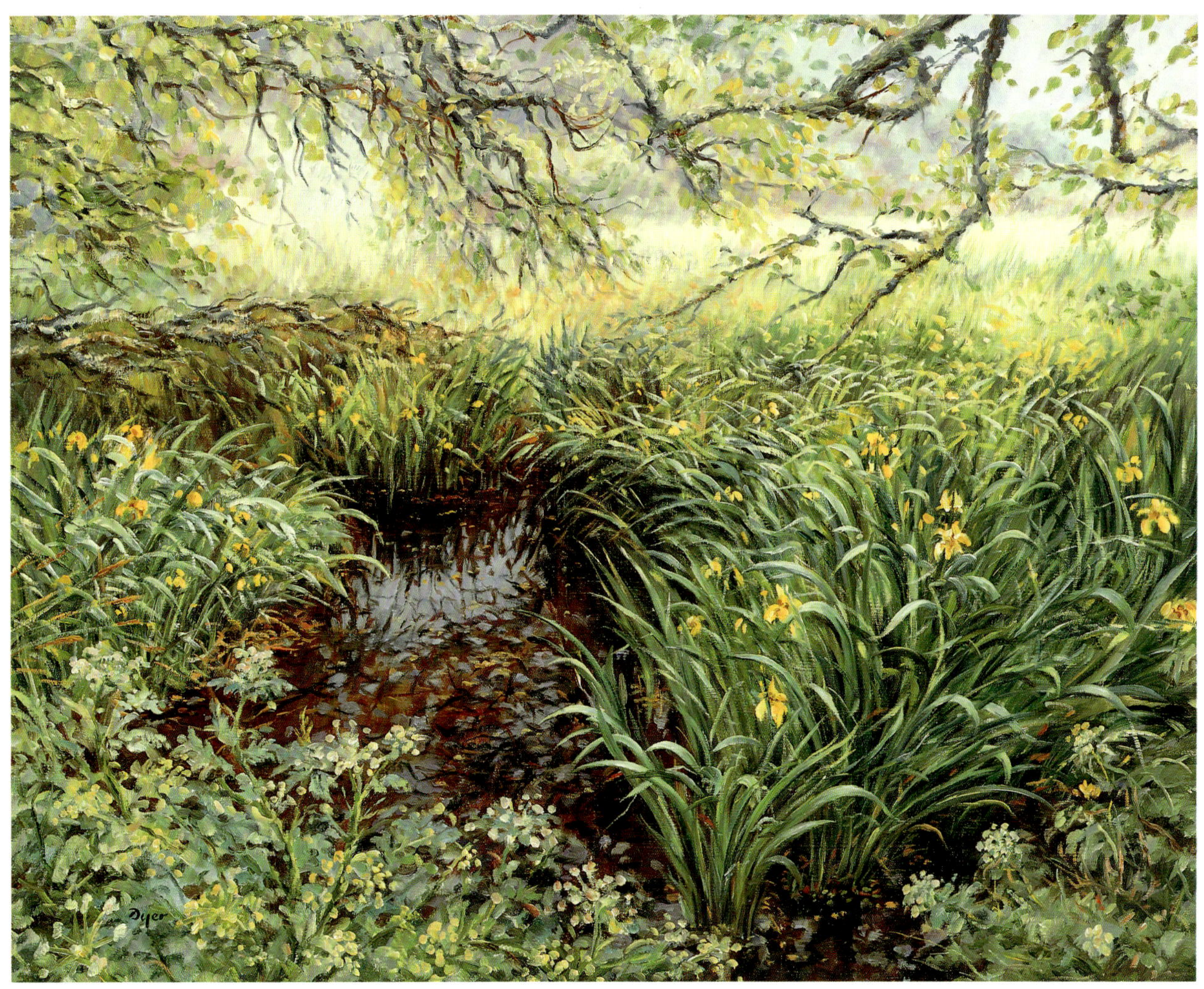

Wild Iris
24 x 30 inches, oil on canvas

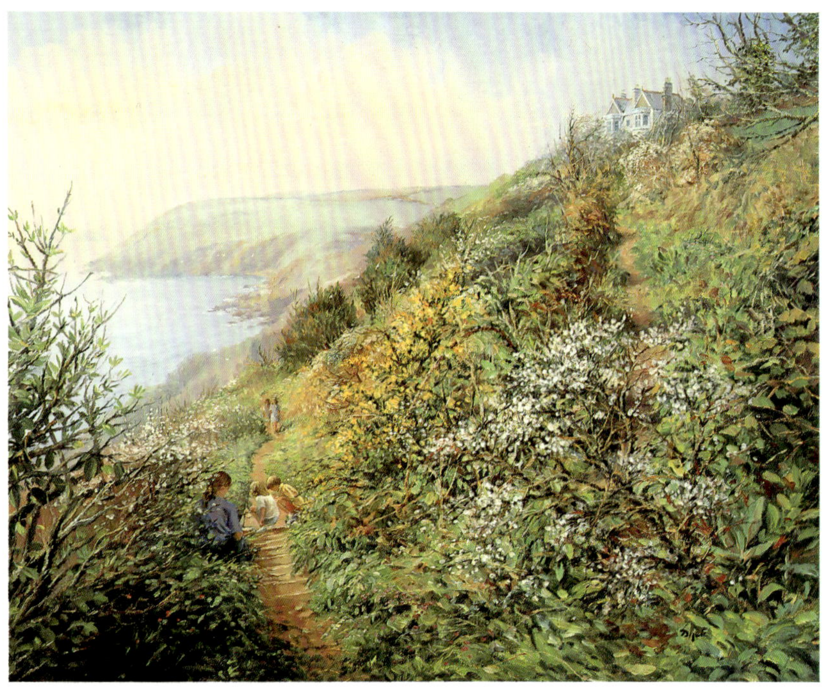

Blackthorn and Gorse, Coastal Path from Port Loe
24 x 30 inches, oil on canvas

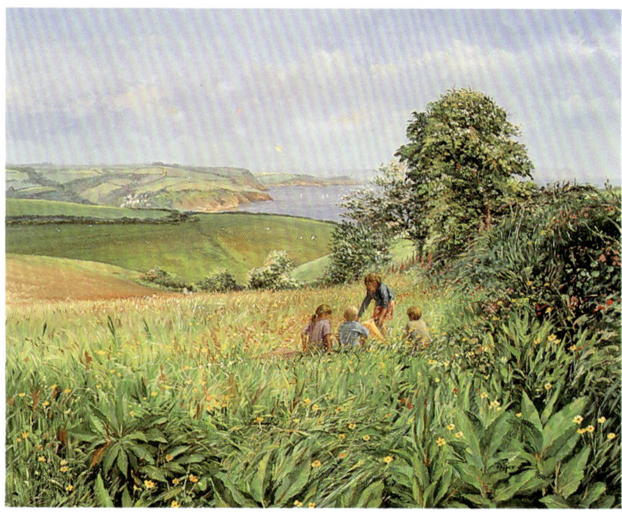

The Buttercup Field
24 x 30 inches, oil on canvas

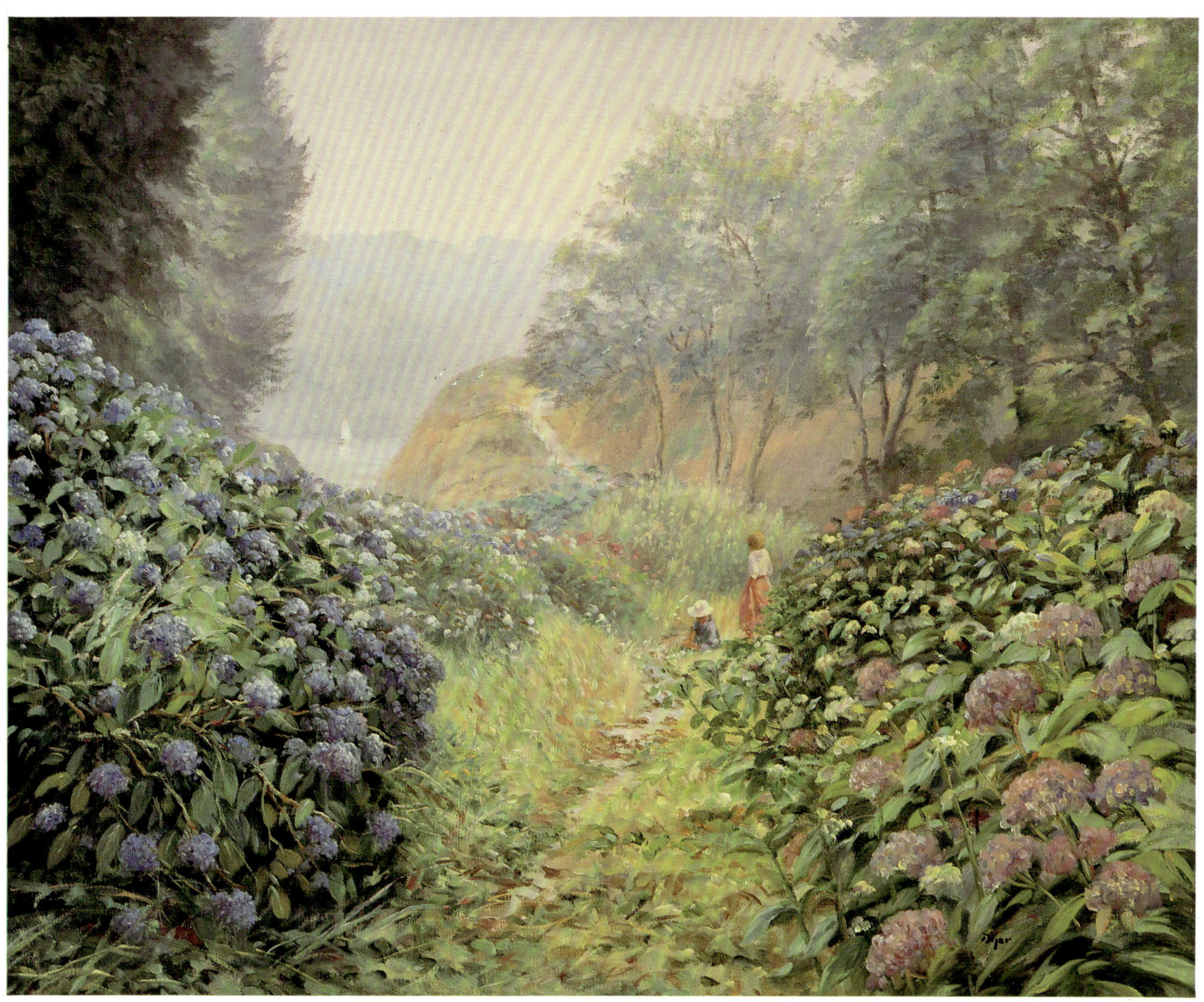

Glorious Hydrangeas, Trebah Gardens
24 x 30 inches, oil on canvas

LOOKING BACK over the paintings that I have produced, the problem of course is not what to include but what not to. A lifetime is far too brief a time to cover my local area, let alone further afield. Perhaps I paint too slowly but it's so easy to be filled with the wonder of a May or June day and not want to explore any further. Still I do miss the blue haze of sleepy heavy summer trees in a slightly more inland location.

It is now nearing the end of the afternoon and I can see sloop rigged yachts returning to their moorings. The wind has increased and the tree immediately outside my studio is swaying gently as its leaves are turned from green to silver as the wind turns them over. There has been sun, showers and now grey sky. How many paintings could have been done I wonder to capture these few hours ? In fact where has the time gone ?

Ted Dyer 1993